USING
THE COMMODORE 64
IN
THE HOME

Hank Librach
Bill L. Behrendt

Micro Text Publications, Inc.
SPECTRUM BOOK Prentice-Hall, Inc., Englewood Cliffs, New Jersey O7632

Librach, Hank
  Using the Commodore 64 in the home.

  "A Spectrum Book."
  1. Commodore 64 (Computer) – Programming.   2. Computer
programs.   I. Behrendt, Bill L.   II. Title.   III. Title:
Using the Commodore sixty-four in the home.
QA76.8.C64L5   1983   001.64   83-9572
ISBN 0-13-940080-X (Prentice-Hall)
ISBN 0-13-940072-9 (Prentice-Hall : pbk.)

To Goldie—thanks for all the work
To Aliza and Ranit for letting me finish on time
—Hank Librach

ISBN 0-13-940072-9 {PBK.}

ISBN 0-13-940099-0 {PBK./DSK.}

This book is available at a special discount when ordered in
bulk quantities. Contact Prentice-Hall, Inc., General
Publishing Division, Special Sales, Englewood Cliffs, N.J. 07632.

Prentice-Hall International, Inc., *London*
Prentice-Hall of Australia Pty. Limited, *Sydney*
Prentice-Hall Canada Inc., *Toronto*
Prentice-Hall of India Private Limited, *New Delhi*
Prentice-Hall of Japan, Inc., *Tokyo*
Prentice-Hall of Southeast Asia Pte. Ltd., *Singapore*
Whitehall Books Limited, *Wellington, New Zealand*
Editora Prentice-Hall do Brasil Ltda., *Rio de Janeiro*

While every precaution has been taken in preparation of the programs of this
book, neither the publisher nor the author will assume any liability resulting
directly or indirectly from use of the programs listed within.

Commodore 64 is a registered trademark of Commodore Business
Machines, Inc.

CONTENTS

INTRODUCTION

COMMODORE 64 IN THE STUDY

COMMODORE 64 IN THE PLAYROOM

APPENDIX

INTRODUCTION

USING THE COMMODORE 64 IN THE HOME offers 20 exciting, original, and easy-to-use programs which can be entered into the Commodore 64 computer directly through the keyboard, without any extra disk or cassette equipment.

These programs cover the whole range of home uses for the Commodore 64: there are programs for financial management, such as checkbook balancers, family budget managers, and loan calculators. There are nutrition planning programs, data management programs which (with storage media) will let you throw away all of your index cards and file cabinets, and educational programs which will catapult your family to the top of their class. There's even an astrology program to entertain friends with, and help you see the future.

And there are games! Ten unique, captivating, amazing games which make use of the astonishing graphics and sound capabilities of the Commodore 64 computer. You can create your own ecological simulation, supervising a whole animal world where only the hardy survive. You can defend a kingdom, travel the outer reaches of space, track down a deadly arsonist, create alien forms of life, and pilot your own plane with a real flight simulator. There are magic mazes to thread your way through, and a program which will teach you more about the sound synthesizing capabilities of the Commodore 64 than you ever thought possible.

And, USING THE COMMODORE 64 IN THE HOME is a highly effective learning-by-using user's guide. Each of the 20 programs is complete with a simple, but extensive, discussion of the programming techniques which went into making up the program. Most BASIC commands are used. By the time you have reviewed and run each program you will be familiar with them. Major concepts are explained, and interesting twists which make especial use of the Commodore 64's unique design are described. All the means are there so that you can modify or elaborate upon the listings to make your own original games.

USING THE COMMODORE 64 IN THE HOME is a long step towards fulfilling for you the promise offered by the new, exciting world of home computing.

COMMODORE 64
IN THE STUDY

1. Nutrition Pack

The importance of good nutrition is generally recognized. This program aids in calculating the calories, proteins and fats in your daily diet. A list of fifty foods is provided from which you can select your daily menu. At the end of your menu selection, a summary of the total number of calories, the total grams of protein and the total grams of fats are displayed.

The program illustrates the use of data arrays, subroutines and display formatting.

An important technique demonstrated in this program is the utilization of arrays. Four arrays are used to contain the nutritional information for each food list. Once a food is chosen, the calorie, protein, and fat contents are stored as individual values. When the user has finished selecting his menu, the total number of calories, grams of protein, and grams of fat are computed and displayed. The array presented consists of fifty different foods which are listed in data statements. The list of foods may be changed to include personal favorites.

TIPS AND TECHNIQUES

- Line 10 clears the screen and prints the heading at a tab of 15 spaces.

- Line 20: The dimension statement sets aside room for four arrays, each consisting of fifty pieces of data. Array variable F$(N) is used for storing the name of the food; notice the $ symbol denoting that it is a string variable containing alpha characters. Array variable C(N) contains information about the caloric content of the respective food. Array variable P(N) contains information about the protein content, and array variable T(N) contains the fat content.

- Lines 30–50: This FOR–NEXT loop reads the elements contained in the data statements in lines 500–990 into the four arrays.

- Line 60 sets up values for a loop, which will display array elements 1 to 20.

- Line 70 executes the display subroutine beginning at line 300. (To be explained.)

- Line 80 sets up parameters to display elements 21 through 40.

- Line 100 sets up parameters to display elements 41 through 50.

- Line 105: This loop is designed to print 12 blank lines and so begin the display midscreen.

- Lines 120–150 display the total number of calories, grams of protein, and fat in the selection.

- Lines 300–380 make up the subroutine that displays a portion of the food array, formats the information into columns, and prompts the user for a food selection.

- Line 300 prints textual column headlines.

- Line 310 sets up a loop which displays an index number N; the food names F$(N); the caloric content C(N); the protein content in grams, P(N); and the fat content in grams, T(N). The array elements to be displayed are determined by the values of A and B, obtained in lines 60, 80, 100. A and B define the beginning and outer limits of the array.

- Line 320 prints the individual element. Notice the way in which the data is arranged in columns. The TAB statement sets up the columns. The index used in the TAB starts counting from the left side of the screen, so TAB (5) is 5 spaces from the left screen edge.

- Line 350 prompts the user to select the number of the food desired. If no selection is desired a zero is entered, in which case the program leaves the subroutine and returns to the line following the call. (Line 80, 100, or 120.) If the value of N is not equal to zero, line 360 is executed next.

- Line 360: This line includes three totalizing counters. Counter C for calorie content, counter P for protein content, and counter T for fat content. The expression $C = C + C(N)$ means the new value of C equals the old value of C plus the value of C(N), the calories for the food chosen.

- Line 370 prompts the user, and if more foods are desired the program branches to line 300 and displays the same block of data. If no more selections are desired then line 380 is executed.

- Line 380: This line is the exit point for the subroutine. Every subroutine must have a return point. The return points in this program are lines 80, 100, and 120.

- Lines 500–990 are the data statements which consist of the food name and three numbers representing the calorie, protein, and fat content. Notice that a precise format must be followed. Each item in the data statement must be separated from the next by a comma. You may substitute your own food preferences and their calorie, protein, and fat contents by replacing the ones provided. If you wish to include more than fifty foods, you need to change the DIM statement in line 20, and the value of B in line 100. Also change the limit of Q in line 105 to display more lines.

VARIABLES USED:

A: Beginning value of element display value.
B: Outer value of element display value.
C(N):   Calorie array element.
F$(N):   Food string array element.
I$:   Selection reply.
N: Array element index.
P(N):   Protein array element.
Q: Counter for screen display position.
T(N):   Fat array element.

PROGRAM LISTING

```
 PRINT CHR$(147);TAB(15)"NUTRITION PACK"
 DIM F$(50),C(50),P(50),T(50)
 FOR N=1 TO 50
 READ F$(N),C(N),P(N),T(N)
 NEXT N
 A=1:B=20
 GOSUB 300
 A=21:B=40
 GOSUB 300
0 A=41:B=50
5 FOR Q=1 TO 12:PRINT:NEXT Q
0 GOSUB 300
0 PRINT CHR$(147)"YOUR FOOD ENERGY AND NUTRIENTS"
0 PRINT"TOTAL CALORIES=";C
0 PRINT"TOTAL PROTEIN(GRAMS)=";P
0 PRINT"TOTAL FAT(GRAMS)=";T
0 END
0 PRINT" #           FOOD          CAL  PRO  FAT"
0 FOR N=A TO B
0 PRINT N;TAB(5);F$(N);TAB(25);C(N);TAB(31);P(N);TAB(35);T(N)
0 NEXT N
0 PRINT
0 INPUT"YOUR SELECTION #(0 FOR NO SELECTION)";N:IF N=0 THEN RETURN
0 C=C+C(N):P=P+P(N):T=T+T(N)
0 PRINT:INPUT"MORE SELECTIONS(Y/N)";I$:IF I$="Y" THEN GOTO 300
0 RETURN
0 DATA APPLE-RAW,80,0,1
0 DATA BACON-2 SLICES,585,4,8
0 DATA BANANA,100,1,0
```

```
530 DATA BEANS-RED 1 CUP,230,15,1
540 DATA BEEF-HAMBURGER 3 OZ,235,20,17
550 DATA BEEF-SIRLOIN 3 OZ,330,20,27
560 DATA BEEF STEW 1 CUP,220,16,11
570 DATA BREAD-RYE 1 SLICE,60,2,0
580 DATA BREAD-WHITE ,70,2,1
590 DATA BUTTER-1 TBSP,100,0,12
600 DATA CAKE-SPONGE SLICE,195,5,4
610 DATA CANTALOUPE-1/2,80,2,0
620 DATA CARROT-1 RAW,30,1,0
630 DATA CATSUP 1 TBSP,15,0,0
640 DATA CHEESE-SWISS 1 OZ,105,8,8
650 DATA CHICKEN-BROIL 3 OZ,115,20,3
660 DATA CORN-1 EAR,70,2,1
670 DATA CORN FLAKES 1 CUP,95,2,0
680 DATA CRACKERS-4 SALTINES,50,1,1
690 DATA DOUGHNUT 1 PLAIN,100,1,5
700 DATA EGG-1 COOKED,80,6,6
710 DATA EGG-OMELET,95,6,7
720 DATA FRANKFURTER,170,7,15
730 DATA FRUIT COCKTAIL-CUP,195,1,0
740 DATA GRAPEFRUIT-1/2 RAW,45,1,0
750 DATA ICE CREAM-1 CUP,270,5,14
760 DATA MACARONI-1 CUP,155,5,1
770 DATA MARGARINE-1 TBSP,100,0,12
780 DATA MAYONNAISE-1 TBSP,100,0,11
790 DATA MILK-SKIM 1 CUP,85,8,0
800 DATA OATMEAL-1 CUP,130,5,2
810 DATA OIL-SALAD 1 TBSP,120,0,14
820 DATA ORANGE-1 MEDIUM,65,1,0
830 DATA ORANGE JUICE 1 CUP,110,2,0
840 DATA OYSTERS RAW -1 CUP,160,20,4
850 DATA PANCAKE WHEAT-1,60,2,2
860 DATA PEANUTBUTTER-1 TBSP,95,4,8
870 DATA PIE-APPLE 4 IN WEDGE,345,3,15
880 DATA PIZZA-CHEESE SLICE,145,6,4
890 DATA POTATOES-BAKED 1,145,4,0
900 DATA POTATO CHIPS-10,115,1,8
910 DATA RICE-WHITE 1 CUP,225,4,0
920 DATA SALAD DRESS-FRENCH,65,0,6
930 DATA SALMON-CAN 3 OZ,120,17,5
940 DATA SARDINES-3 OZ,175,20,9
950 DATA SPAGHETTI-1 CUP,155,5,1
960 DATA SUGAR-1 TEASPOON,15,0,0
970 DATA TOMATO JUICE-1 CUP,45,2,0
980 DATA TUNA FISH-3 OZ,170,24,7
990 DATA YOGURT-LOFAT PLAIN,145,12,4
```

2. Family Budget Comptroller

If you are having difficulty determining where your family income is going and would like to better monitor family expenditures, this program will provide you with an opportunity to analyze your expenses. The program has provisions for 15 predefined expense categories. You enter your allocation into each category. You also enter your total income for the period. The program will then return your final balance. It will also display your total expenses and warn you if your balance is in the red.

This program illustrates the use of subscripted variables, and display formatting of tabular data. You are also introduced to the LEN, length, and STR$, string, functions.

TIPS AND TECHNIQUES

- Line 10 clears the screen and presents the program title.

- Line 20: This line sets up room for two arrays. Array N will hold fifteen elements. They are the amounts spent in each category. Array N$ is also composed of fifteen elements. They are the fifteen categories. Since they contain alphabetic information the string symbol, $, is used.

- Line 30 prompts the user for the total income.

- Lines 40–180 contain 15 categories of expenses. You may change the categories if you wish.

- Line 200 prompts the user to enter expenses.

- Lines 210–250 set up a FOR-NEXT loop, which prints the expense headings, and prompts the user to input the amounts budgeted. Notice the use of the subscripted variable N(C), which holds the amount of the item N$(C).

- Lines 260–280: This FOR-NEXT loop sums the expenses using variable T. After all 15 categories have been summed the total of the expenses is obtained.

- Line 290: This line solves for the balance B.

- Line 300 clears the screen.

- Line 310 prints the total income which was assigned to variable I in line 30.

- Lines 330–360 set up a FOR-NEXT loop which displays a summary of the expenses.

- Line 350 formats the display of the screen. At column 10 on the screen the category name is displayed, the cursor moves to the right side of the screen to display the amounts. The variable X is the amount budgeted for a particular item. In order to align all the numbers in a column, the following technique is used: you convert the number X into a string variable using the STR$ function. You can now determine how many characters that numerical answer consists of. This helps determine in which column to print the number so that the display aligns and looks neat. The string function LEN determines how many digits are in the answer. By subtracting 38 from this number you tab the cursor the resultant number of spaces and print the value of X. This process is repeated 15 times for each category.

- Line 370 prints the sum of the expenses.

- Line 380 prints the final balance.

- Line 390: If the balance equals zero or is less than zero, you are advised to start saving.

VARIABLES USED:

B: Amount of balance.
C: Index in a FOR-NEXT loop.
I: Total income.
J: Index in a FOR-Next loop.
N: Subscripted variable storing the amounts.
N$: Subscripted variables storing category names.
T: Sum of expenses.
X: Used for TAB position.

PROGRAM LISTING

```
10 PRINT CHR$(147),"FAMILY BUDGET ANALYSIS"
20 DIM N(15),N$(15)
30 PRINT:INPUT"TOTAL INCOME(PER WEEK/OR PER MONTH):$";I
40 N$(1)="FOOD:"
50 N$(2)="RENT/MORTGAGE:"
60 N$(3)="MEDICAL:"
70 N$(4)="INSURANCE:"
80 N$(5)="TAXES:"
90 N$(6)="EDUCATION:"
100 N$(7)="AUTOMOBILE(GAS/REPAIR):"
110 N$(8)="HEAT(OIL /GAS):"
120 N$(9)="ELECTRICITY:"
130 N$(10)="TELEPHONE:"
140 N$(11)="CLOTHING:"
150 N$(12)="ALLOWANCES:"
160 N$(13)="MAINTENANCE(HOME):"
170 N$(14)="ENTERTAINMENT:"
180 N$(15)="OTHERS:"
190 PRINT
200 PRINT"ENTER EXPENSES FOR THE FOLLOWING ITEMS:"
210 FOR C=1 TO 15
220 PRINT
230 PRINT N$(C)
240 INPUT "AMOUNT=$";N(C)
250 NEXT C
260 FOR C=1 TO 15
270 T=T+N(C)
280 NEXT C
290 B=I-T
300 PRINT CHR$(147)
310 PRINT"TOTAL INCOME=";I
320 PRINT:PRINT"EXPENSES="
330 FOR J=1 TO 15
340 X=N(J)
350 PRINT TAB(10);N$(J);TAB(38-LEN(STR$(X)));X
360 NEXT J
370 PRINT:PRINT"TOTAL EXPENSES=$";T
380 PRINT"BALANCE=$";B
390 IF B<=0 THEN PRINT"START SAVING!"
```

SAVE "JANICE ", 8

LOAD "$", 8

LOAD "JANICE", 8

3. Shakespeare!

This program gives you an opportunity to review your knowledge of the parts of speech while creating amusing rhymes. After you have typed in the parts of speech requested by the program, a somewhat familiar rhyme is generated. There are five different rhyme modules, any one of which will be randomly selected by the program. This program introduces random numbers and string variables.

You may wish to review these definitions:

Noun: a word denoting a person, place or thing.
Verb: a word denoting action.
Adjective: a word describing a noun.

TIPS AND TECHNIQUES

- Lines 20–40: These lines display the opening prompt describing the program.

- Line 50 generates a random number between 1 and 5. Since the random function RND generates a value between 0 and 1, you multiply it by 5, take the integer part of the answer with the INT function, and add 1 to the final answer. This technique assures you of generating a random number between the lower limit of 1 and some upper limit. In this case the upper limit is 5.

- Line 60: This line, depending on the value of N (the random number), picks the rhyme to be displayed. If N = 1 the program branches to line 100; if N = 2 the program branches to line 200; and if N = 5 the program branches to line 500.

- Lines 100–150 prompt the user for the parts of speech. Notice that since you are entering non-numerical information, each input is accepted as a string variable.

- Line 160 sends the program to line 600. In lines 600–630 the composed rhyme is generated. It is built from the string variables that were entered earlier.

- Lines 200–260 request the parts of speech required for the second rhyme.

- Line 270 starts the generation of the second rhyme by branching to line 650.

- Lines 300–370 request the parts of speech for the third rhyme.

- Line 380 starts the generation of the third rhyme by branching to line 700.

- Lines 400–450 request the parts of speech for the fourth rhyme.

- Line 460 starts the generation of the fourth rhyme by branching to line 760.

- Lines 500–560 request the parts of speech for the fifth rhyme.

- Line 570 starts the generation of the fifth rhyme by branching to line 810.

- Lines 600–630: These lines display the first rhyme.

- Line 640 sends the program to a routine beginning at line 900.

- Line 900 asks if the user wishes to run the program again.

- Line 910: If the reply is yes, the program branches to line 50 which generates a new random number.

- Lines 650–680: These lines display the second rhyme.

- Lines 700–740: These lines display the third rhyme.

- Lines 760–790: These lines display the fourth rhyme.

- Lines 810–840: These lines display the fifth rhyme.

VARIABLES USED:

Each variable is a string variable storing user input.

PROGRAM LISTING

```
10 PRINT CHR$(147),"POETRY GENERATOR":PRINT
20 INPUT"WHAT IS YOUR NAME ";A$:PRINT
30 PRINT"DEAR "A$" WE ARE GOING TO GENERATE "
40 PRINT"POETRY BUT I WILL NEED YOUR HELP-SO GIVE ME:":PRINT
50 N=INT(5*(RND(1)))+1
60 ON N GOTO 100,200,300,400,500
100 INPUT"A GIRLS NAME";B$
110 INPUT"A NOUN";C$
120 INPUT"A FOOD";D$
130 INPUT"A NOUN THAT RHYMES WITH 'DAY'";E$
140 INPUT"A NOUN";F$
150 INPUT"A PREPOSITION";G$
160 GOTO 600
200 INPUT"A NAME";H$
210 INPUT"AN ADJECTIVE";I$
220 INPUT"AN ANIMAL";J$
230 INPUT"A NOUN";K$
240 INPUT"A COLOR";L$
250 INPUT"A NOUN";M$
260 INPUT"A VERB THAT RHYMES WITH 'SNOW'";N$
270 GOTO 650
300 INPUT"A NUMBER";O$
310 INPUT"AN ADJECTIVE";P$
320 INPUT"AN ANIMAL(PLURAL)";Q$
330 INPUT"A VERB";R$
340 INPUT"A NOUN";S$
350 INPUT"PLURAL NOUN";T$
360 INPUT"A NOUN";U$
370 INPUT"AN ADJECTIVE";V$
380 GOTO 700
400 INPUT"AN ADJECTIVE";W$
410 INPUT"A BOYS NAME";X$
420 INPUT"AN ADJECTIVE";Y$
430 INPUT"A NOUN";Z$
440 INPUT"A NOUN";AA$
450 INPUT"A NOUN";AB$
460 GOTO 760
500 INPUT"A BOYS NAME";AC$
510 INPUT"A GIRLS NAME";AD$
520 INPUT"A NOUN";AE$
530 INPUT"A CONTAINER NAME";AF$
540 INPUT"A LIQUID";AG$
550 INPUT"A NOUN";AH$
560 INPUT"A VERB";AI$
570 GOTO 810
600 PRINT CHR$(147):PRINT"LITTLE MISS "B$" SAT ON A "C$","
610 PRINT"EATING HER "D$" AND "E$"."
620 PRINT"ALONG CAME A "F$" AND SAT DOWN "G$" HER"
630 PRINT"AND FRIGHTENED MISS "B$" AWAY."
640 GOTO 900
650 PRINT CHR$(147):PRINT H$" HAD A "I$" "J$"."
660 PRINT"ITS "K$" WAS "L$" AS SNOW."
670 PRINT"AND EVERYWHERE THAT "H$" WENT"
680 PRINT"HER "M$" WAS SURE TO "N$"."
690 GOTO 900
700 PRINT CHR$(147):PRINT O$" "P$" "Q$". SEE HOW THEY "R$"!"
710 PRINT"THEY ALL RAN AFTER THE FARMER'S "S$","
```

```
720 PRINT"WHO CUT OFF THEIR "T$" WITH A CARVING "U$"."
730 PRINT"DID YOU EVER SEE SUCH A SIGHT IN YOUR LIFE"
740 PRINT"AS "O$" "V$" "Q$"?"
750 GOTO 900
760 PRINT CHR$(147):PRINT W$" "X$" SAT IN A CORNER"
770 PRINT"EATING HIS "Y$" PIE."
780 PRINT"HE STUCK IN HIS "Z$" AND PULLED OUT A "AA$
790 PRINT"AND SAID,WHAT A GOOD "AB$" AM I!"
800 GOTO 900
810 PRINT CHR$(147):PRINT AC$" AND "AD$" WENT UP THE "AE$
820 PRINT"TO GET A "AF$" OF "AG$"."
830 PRINT AC$" FELL DOWN AND BROKE HIS "AH$","
840 PRINT"AND "AD$" CAME "AI$;"ING AFTER."
900 PRINT:PRINT:INPUT"WANT TO TRY ANOTHER ONE(Y/N)";AJ$
910 IF AJ$="Y"    THEN GOTO 50
920 PRINT"HAVE A NICE DAY"
```

4. Commodore Checkbook Keeper

The woes of checkbook balancing have long plagued many of us. If you find you are often faced with this frustrating problem, consider turning to this program for help. A summary of your checkbook transactions totaling all deposits, all outstanding checks and all checks made is presented. A final balance is displayed and the user is warned if the balance dips below zero. The program is user friendly; all user inputs are prompted. In fact, this program is self-contained and no other calculating devices are required. The program is written with simple statements at each line, instead of multiple statements per line, thus facilitating analysis of program development.

The program illustrates the following programming techniques: branching, menu displays, summation with variables, subroutines, and the use of inequalities.

TIPS AND TECHNIQUES

- Line 10 clears the screen and displays the program title.

- Line 20: The PRINT statement alone prints a blank line on the display. This is done to create a more readable and visually pleasing display.

- Lines 30–40 instruct the user on selecting one of the options available.

- Lines 60–140 display the five options that are available to the user.

- Line 160 prompts the user to enter the option number.

- Line 170: This line checks to see if the user's reply is in the range of 1 to 5. This line reads as follows: If the value of N is greater than 5 or if the value of N is less than 1, then print the following message "ENTER CORRECT NUMBER." If either of the conditions is met the program returns to line 160. If neither condition is met the program advances to line 180.

- Line 180: If the input is a number between 1 and 5 the program reaches this line, which sends the program to one of five different routines depending on the number entered. If N = 1 the program branches to line 300; if N = 2 it branches to line 350 and if N = 5 it branches to line 500.

- Line 300: This is the module which accepts data regarding deposits. The program immediately branches to a subroutine at line 700 which will be considered shortly.

- Line 310 prompts the user to enter data regarding deposits.

- Line 320: The amounts of the deposits are summed to variable S. As each new deposit is entered into variable D, it is added to S. In this manner a summation of variable D is performed. This simulates calculator addition.

- Line 330 sends the program back to line 300, which then sends the program to a subroutine at line 700. Let's examine what the subroutine at line 700 does.

The subroutine consists of line 700 to 770.

- Line 700 tells the user how to enter new data.

- Line 710 tells the user how to see the menu again.

- Line 740 accepts the user's choice as variable Z$, which is a string variable since the answer consists of letters.

- Line 750: If the user chooses to enter more data, the program returns from the subroutine; the return point is the line following the GOSUB instruction.

- Line 760: If the user chooses to see the menu, the screen is cleared.

- Line 770: The program branches back to line 20.

Let us review the routine at line 300. If we want to enter more data for "DEPOSITS" for example, the subroutine at line 700 sends the program back to line 310. At line 330 if we want to continue entering data, the program again goes to line 300.

- Lines 350–380 follow a format similar to the above in summing the checks made.

- Lines 400–430 sum the outstanding checks.

- Lines 450–480 sum the service charges.

- Lines 500–620 print the summation for each category.

- Line 630 calculates the balance. It is computed by adding the balance to the deposits and subtracting the value of the checks written and the amount of outstanding checks in addition to subtracting the total service charge.

- Line 660 prints the balance.

- Line 670 alerts the user if the balance is less than zero.

- Line 680 ends the program. This line is necessary to prevent the program from running into the subroutine starting at line 700, in which case the computer would display an error message.

VARIABLES USED:

B: Balance in the checking account.
C: Value of check.
D: Amount of deposits.
E: Total amount for service charges.
G: Amount of outstanding checks.
N: Option choice.
R: Total value of outstanding checks.
S: Total amount deposited.
T: Total value of checks written.
V: Amount of service charge.
Z$:   User response to question.

PROGRAM LISTING

```
10 PRINT CHR$(147),"CHECKBOOK MANAGER"
20 PRINT
30 PRINT"SELECT YOUR OPTION BY TYPING"
40 PRINT"THE CORRESPONDING NUMBER"
50 PRINT
60 PRINT"1: DEPOSITS MADE"
70 PRINT
80 PRINT"2: CHECKS MADE"
90 PRINT
100 PRINT"3: OUTSTANDING CHECKS"
110 PRINT
120 PRINT"4: SERVICE CHARGES"
130 PRINT
140 PRINT"5: END PROGRAM-SEE TOTAL SUMMARY"
150 PRINT
160 INPUT"YOUR OPTION NUMBER IS:";N
170 IF (N>5) OR (N<1) THEN PRINT"ENTER CORRECT NUMBER!":GOTO 160
180 ON N GOTO 300,350,400,450,500
```

```
300 GOSUB 700
310 INPUT"DEPOSITS=";D
320 S=S+D
330 GOTO 300
350 GOSUB 700
360 INPUT"CHECKS MADE";C
370 T=T+C
380 GOTO 350
400 GOSUB 700
410 INPUT"OUTSTANDING CHECKS";G
420 R=R+G
430 GOTO 400
450 GOSUB 700
460 INPUT"SERVICE CHARGES";V
470 E=E+V
480 GOTO 450
500 PRINT CHR$(147)
510 INPUT"BALANCE AT START=";B
520 PRINT CHR$(147),"CHECKBOOK SUMMARY"
530 PRINT
540 PRINT"STARTING BALANCE=$";B
550 PRINT
560 PRINT"TOTAL DEPOSITS=$";S
570 PRINT
580 PRINT"TOTAL OF ALL CHECKS MADE=$";T
590 PRINT
600 PRINT"TOTAL OF OUTSTANDING CHECKS=$";R
610 PRINT
620 PRINT"TOTAL SERVICE CHARGES=$";E
630 B=B+S-T+R-E
640 PRINT
650 PRINT
660 PRINT"BALANCE=$";B
670 IF B<0 THEN PRINT"YOU ARE IN THE RED-START SAVING!"
680 END
700 PRINT
710 PRINT"TYPE 'E' TO ENTER NEW DATA"
720 PRINT
730 PRINT"TYPE 'Q' TO SEE MENU AGAIN"
735 PRINT
740 INPUT"YOUR OPTION(E OR Q)";Z$
750 IF Z$="E" THEN RETURN
760 PRINT CHR$(147)
770 GOTO 20
```

5. The Fortune Teller

What is your sign?

Here is a program you can have fun with at your next party. You select a number from the display menu corresponding to your birthdate. Your astrological sign and personality characteristics are displayed. The program is easy to use. All input is prompted and the results are fun to interpret.

This program introduces two dimensional arrays, READ-DATA statements, and nested FOR-NEXT loops.

TIPS AND TECHNIQUES

The program utilizes two arrays. One array stores the signs of the zodiac and the other array stores six dominant characteristics for each sign. Different traits are given for males and females. Once the number corresponding to your birthdate is selected, all retrieved data is indexed to that number. Array M$ is a two dimensional array. It stores 6 male characteristics for each sign of the zodiac, and 6 female characteristics for each sign of the zodiac. In total this array holds $24 \times 6 = 144$ pieces of information. We shall see how the correct data is retrieved.

- Line 10 sets up the M and K arrays. Since they store alphabetic data the string symbol $ is used with the array name.

- Lines 20–130 display the months and corresponding number.

- Line 170 checks to see if the number entered is greater than 12. If it is you are reminded that you can only select the numbers 1–12.

- Line 200 prompts the user to indicate his sex.

- Line 210 sends the program to subroutines reading the male characteristics into an array and then displaying the information.

- Line 220 sends the program to subroutines reading the female characteristics into an array and then displaying the information.

- Line 240: Another error trapping routine. If your reply to line 200 is neither an M or an F the program returns to line 200.

- Lines 300–450: This subroutine reads the signs of the zodiac into array K$.

- Lines 300–320: This FOR-NEXT loop reads the 12 astrological signs and stores this information in array K$.

- Lines 330–440 are the data statements containing the 12 signs of the zodiac.

- Line 450 ends the subroutine.

- Lines 500–540: This nested FOR-NEXT loop reads into an array the 24 categories with 6 characteristics in each category. These are the male and female attributes for each sign.

- Line 520: Notice the subscripts for array M$. They are variable I which goes from 1 to 6. We first read the I = 1 value for the values of J = 1 to 6. This means that we first read all elements in line 550. Next I = 2 and again we read 6 elements. These would be in line 560, and so forth.

- Lines 530–540: Notice the order of the next element to be read. After 6 elements are read into the array the next I element is read.

- Lines 550–890 are data statements with the information for the attribute array. Notice that the attributes are separated by commas.

- Line 900: The return statement ends the subroutine and returns the program to line 210 or 220.

- Line 910: Using the value of N (from line 160) your sign is printed from array K$(N).

- Lines 920–940 print the traits attributed to the birthdate indicated for males. These are from the data elements in lines 500–670.

- Line 950 ends the program after 6 male attributes have been displayed.

- Lines 960–980 print the traits attributed to the birthdate indicated for females. The data statements in lines 750–780 provide this information. Notice in line 980 that the first subscript in the M$ matrix is N + 12, which corresponds to elements 13 to 24 in the data matrix.

- Line 1000 ends the program after six female attributes have been printed.

VARIABLES USED:

A$: User reponse indicating sex.
I: Index for position in attribution matrix.
J: Index for attribute.
K: Sign array index.
K$: Sign array.
M$: A two dimensional array.
N: Birth date index.

PROGRAM LISTING

```
10 DIM M$(24,6),K$(12)
15 PRINT CHR$(147),"SIGNS OF THE ZODIAC":PRINT
20 PRINT"1 : 21 MARCH TO 19 APRIL"
30 PRINT"2 : 20 APRIL TO 20 MAY"
40 PRINT"3 : 21 MAY   TO 20 JUNE"
50 PRINT"4 : 21 JUNE  TO 22 JULY"
60 PRINT"5 : 23 JULY  TO 22 AUGUST"
70 PRINT"6 : 23 AUGUST TO 22 SEPTEMBER"
80 PRINT"7 : 23 SEPTEMBER TO 22 OCTOBER"
90 PRINT"8 : 23 OCTOBER TO 21 NOVEMBER"
100 PRINT"9 : 22 NOVEMBER TO 21 DECEMBER"
110 PRINT"10: 22 DECEMBER TO 19 JANUARY"
120 PRINT"11: 20 JANUARY TO 18 FEBRUARY"
130 PRINT"12: 19 FEBRUARY TO 20 MARCH"
140 PRINT:PRINT"ENTER THE NUMBER CORRESPONDING TO"
150 PRINT"YOUR BIRTH DATE (1-12)"
160 INPUT "#=";N
170 IF N>12 THEN PRINT"ENTER (1-12) ONLY":GOTO 160
180 PRINT:PRINT"OBTAIN SIGNS OF THE ZODIAC FOR:"
190 PRINT"A MALE,OR A FEMALE"
200 INPUT"TYPE: M OR F ";A$
210 IF A$="M" THEN GOSUB 300:GOSUB 500:GOTO 910
220 IF A$="F" THEN GOSUB 300:GOSUB 500:GOTO 960
240 PRINT"YOU MUST BE ONE OF THE ABOVE":GOTO 200
300 FOR K=1 TO 12
310 READ K$(K)
320 NEXT K
330 DATA ARIES- THE RAM
340 DATA TAURUS-THE BULL
350 DATA GEMINI-THE TWINS
360 DATA CANCER-THE CRAB
370 DATA LEO-THE LION
380 DATA VIRGO-THE VIRGIN
390 DATA LIBRA-THE SCALES
400 DATA SCORPIO-THE SCORPION
410 DATA SAGITTARIUS-THE ARCHER
420 DATA CAPRICORN-THE GOAT
430 DATA AQUARIUS-THE WATER CARRIER
440 DATA  PISCES-THE FISH
450 RETURN
500 FOR I=1 TO 24
510 FOR J=1 TO 6
520 READ M$(I,J)
```

```
30 NEXT J
40 NEXT I
50 DATA FAITHFUL,IDEALISTIC,POSSESSIVE,JEALOUS,DEMANDING,SENTIMENTAL
60 DATA STRONG,CONSIDERATE,WANTS SECURITY,LOVES HOME,LOYAL,ROMANTIC
70 DATA UNPREDICTABLE,IMAGINATIVE,ACTIVE,LACK OF PATIENCE,WITTY
75 DATA TALKER
80 DATA LOYAL,FICKLE,ARTISTIC,GOOD FATHER,LOVES HOME,ORGANIZER
90 DATA DOMINANT,JEALOUS,FLIRTS,LOYAL,AFFECTIONATE,GENEROUS
10 DATA LOYAL,DECENT,UNDEMONSTRATIVE,POSSESSIVE,STRICT,PRECISE
20 DATA LIKES SECURITY,COURTEOUS,OBLIGING,SOCIABLE,IDEALISTIC,LAZY
30 DATA ENERGETIC,SELF-INDULGENT,RECKLESS,IMAGINATIVE,SUBTLE
35 DATA SECRETIVE
40 DATA OPTIMISTIC,IDEALISTIC,INTELLIGENT,NOT JEALOUS,HONEST
45 DATA OPEN MINDED
50 DATA CAREFUL,SERIOUS,CONSCIENTIOUS,AMBITIOUS,RELIABLE,GOOD LEADER
60 DATA ECCENTRIC,FRIENDLY,SYMPATHETIC,IDEALISTIC,ALOOF
65 DATA CONSTANTLY ANALYZING
70 DATA SYMPATHETIC,KIND,SENSITIVE,RECEPTIVE,MOODY,A DREAMER
80 DATA INDEPENDENT,OPTIMISTIC,IDEALISTIC,SENTIMENTAL,LOYAL
85 DATA A CAREER WOMAN
90 DATA STEADFAST,LOYAL,EASYGOING,WARM HEART,EMOTIONAL,BEAUTY
00 DATA FICKLE,CHARM,A THINKER,GOOD IMAGINATION,LIVELY,MOODY
10 DATA MOTHERLY,PROTECTIVE,IMAGINATIVE,SENSITIVE,MOODY
15 DATA  GOOD AT SAVING
20 DATA POPULAR,GOOD LOOKING,LIKES FINE CLOTHES,INTELLIGENT
30 DATA GOOD SENSE OF HUMOR,INDEPENDENT
40 DATA PRACTICAL,LOVING,ORDERLY,EFFICIENT,LOYAL,ARTISTIC
50 DATA INTELLECTUAL,WITTY,CHARMING,SENTIMENTAL,AFFECTIONATE
55 DATA WORK ALONE
60 DATA POSSESSIVE,LOYAL,AFFECTIONATE,LOOKS FOR A STRONG PARTNER
70 DATA BURNS WITH JEALOUSY,KEEPS A CLEAN HOME
80 DATA CHEERFUL,OPTIMISTIC,HAPPY GO LUCKY,FRIENDLY,HONEST,CONFIDENT
90 DATA SENSIBLE,DETERMINED,CLEVER,SUPERIOR,AMBITIOUS,GOOD WIFE
00 DATA POISED,FAITHFUL,A GOOD HOSTESS,HELPS FRIENDS
05 DATA WILL NOT BE TIED DOWN
10 DATA WORK WHEN MARRIED
20 DATA WITTY,PRETTY,FEMININE,SECRETIVE,DECEPTIVE,DREAMY
30 RETURN
0 PRINT CHR$(147):PRINT K$(N),"(MALE TRAITS)":  PRINT
10 FOR J=1 TO 6
20 PRINT M$(N,J):PRINT
40 NEXT J
70 END
0 PRINT CHR$(147):PRINT K$(N),"(FEMALE TRAITS)":PRINT
90 FOR J=1 TO 6
00 PRINT M$(N+12,J):PRINT
10 NEXT J
00 END
```

6. Money Manager

In dealing with today's turbulent economic picture, it is important to take advantage of all possible aids and advice. Money Manager can help you by providing you with the means of analyzing possible investments. It will help you with such matters as calculating the future value of an investment given the present value, calculating the length of time to invest and the length of time it will take for an investment to double.

This program consists of four options. Each option can serve as a separate module. The options are:

Option 1: Find the future value of an investment. For example, given $4000.00 invested at 8% compounded annually for 10 years, this option will calculate the future value.

Option 2: Calculates the amount you must invest today in order to accrue a certain amount by a future date. For example it will calculate the amount to be invested today at 9% compounded annually in order to accrue $10,000 in 10 years.

Option 3: Calculates the amount of interest paid during the investment period and will find what the compound interest is on $10,000 for 2 years if interest is 8% and compounded annually.

Option 4: Solves for the time required for an investment. For example—how long does it take $5000.00 to double if it is invested at 10% annual interest compounded annually? One caution should be observed when dealing with financial calculations. The time periods and interest rates should be in consistent time units. The above examples are all for annual compounding of interest. However, if you wish, say, to compound quarterly at an 8% annual interest rate then the interest, or I, would be 8/4 for each quarter.

The program is self-prompting and each module can stand alone. The program illustrates the use of subroutines where repeated text is displayed.

TIPS AND TECHNIQUES

- Line 10 clears the screen.

- Lines 30–120 display the options available.

- Line 150 prompts the user to select the desired option.

- Line 160 checks to see if the user made an incorrect choice. If the number selected is greater than 4, the user is reminded to select a number from 1 to 4. Line 150 prompts the user again.

- Line 170: When a number in the range of 1 to 4 is selected, a branch to the corresponding module takes place. If module #1 is chosen A = 1 and the program branches to line 300. If module #4 is chosen A = 4 and the program branches to line 600.

- Line 190 asks the user if more calculations are desired.

- Line 200: If the answer is a Y for yes, the program returns to line 10, and the menu is displayed again.

- Line 210: If the response is an N, the program ends. Notice the END statement. It is essential here so that the program will not execute subsequent lines which are subroutines.

- Lines 300–380 comprise the first module.

- Line 310 displays the title.

- Line 320 branches to a subroutine at line 800.

- Line 800 accepts the value for P and returns the program to line 330.

- Line 330 sends the program to a subroutine at line 820.

- Line 820 accepts the value for I and converts the value of I into a percentage and then returns the program to line 340.

- Line 340 sends the program to another subroutine at line 830.

- Line 830 accepts the value for N and returns the program to line 350.

- Line 350 solves the equation for the future value.

- Line 360 calls for a subroutine beginning at line 900 to round the answer to two decimal places.

- Lines 900–930 contains a subroutine to round the answer to two places. This is essential in order to display the cents part of the calculated value to two places.

- Line 370 displays the answer rounded to two decimal places.

- Line 380 branches back to line 180.

- Lines 400–480 comprise the second option.

- Lines 500–580 perform the calculations for the third option.

- Lines 600–690 perform the calculations for the fourth option.

Notice that all the modules follow the same format. By studying the first module you should be able to trace the remaining modules.

VARIABLES USED:

A: The selection choice, also the integer part of the answer.
A\$: Used to ask the user if more options are desired.
C: The fractional part of the answer rounded to two places.
D: Totals the integer and the decimal part of the calculations.
F: Future value.
I: Interest value.
K: Dummy variable. Used to pass values.
N: Investment time value.
P: Present value.
Q: Counter for display.
T: Total interest value.

PROGRAM LISTING

```
10 PRINT CHR$(147):PRINT
20 PRINT TAB(15)"MONEY MAKER":PRINT
30 PRINT"OPTION #1"
40 PRINT"FIND THE FUTURE VALUE OF AN INVESTMENT"
50 PRINT
60 PRINT"OPTION #2"
70 PRINT"FIND THE AMOUNT TO INVEST NOW"
80 PRINT
90 PRINT"OPTION #3"
100 PRINT"FIND THE TOTAL INTEREST PAID"
110 PRINT
120 PRINT"OPTION #4"
130 PRINT"FIND THE TIME DURATION OF AN INVESTMENT"
140 PRINT:PRINT
150 INPUT"SELECT YOUR OPTION (1-4)";A
160 IF A>4 THEN PRINT"ENTER OPTION #(1-4)":GOTO 150
170 ON A GOTO 300,400,500,600
180 FOR Q=1 TO 4:PRINT:NEXT Q
```

```
190 INPUT"ANY MORE CALCULATIONS (Y/N)";A$
200 IF A$="Y" THEN GOTO 10
210 END
300 PRINT CHR$(147):PRINT
310 PRINT"FIND FUTURE VALUE":PRINT
320 GOSUB 800
330 GOSUB 820
340 GOSUB 830
350 F=P*(1+I)↑N
360 K=F:GOSUB 900:F=D
370 PRINT:PRINT"FUTURE VALUE=$";F
380 GOTO 180
400 PRINT CHR$(147):PRINT
410 PRINT"FIND PRESENT VALUE":PRINT
420 GOSUB 810
430 GOSUB 820
440 GOSUB 830
450 P=F*(1+I)↑-N
460 K=P:GOSUB 900:P=D
470 PRINT:PRINT"PRESENT VALUE=$";P
480 GOTO 180
500 PRINT CHR$(147):PRINT
510 PRINT"FIND TOTAL INTEREST":PRINT
520 GOSUB 800
530 GOSUB 820
540 GOSUB 830
550 T=P*((1+I)↑N-1)
560 K=T:GOSUB 900:T=D
570 PRINT:PRINT"INTEREST PAID=$";T
580 GOTO 180
600 PRINT CHR$(147):PRINT
610 PRINT"FIND TIME DURATION OF AN INVESTMENT":PRINT
620 GOSUB 800
630 GOSUB 810
640 GOSUB 820
650 N=LOG(F/P)/LOG(1+I)
660 PRINT"(UNITS ARE CONSISTENT WITH INTEREST RATE TIME UNITS) "
670 K=N:GOSUB 900:N=D
680 PRINT"TIME=";N
690 GOTO 180
800 PRINT:INPUT"PRESENT VALUE=$";P:RETURN
810 PRINT:INPUT"FUTURE VALUE=$";F:RETURN
820 PRINT:INPUT"INTEREST %=";I:I=.01*I:RETURN
830 PRINT:INPUT"INPUT TIME=";N:RETURN
900 A=INT(K):B=K-A
910 C=INT(B*100+.5)/100
920 D=A+C
930 RETURN
```

7. Your Math Teacher

Are you or any members of your family having difficulty with arithmetic? This program helps you practice and improve your arithmetic skills. You may elect to practice addition, subtraction, multiplication, or division, or concentrate on a specific multiplication table. In order to accomodate different ability levels the user can select the highest integer desired and the number of questions to be presented. If the questions are answered correctly the program offers positive reinforcement. If the answer is incorrect, the correct answer is shown. At the end of the quiz the number of problems correctly answered is displayed.

The program consists of five modules and a number of subroutines. Each option can serve as an independent module. The random number function is used to generate the digits for each problem. The INT integer function is also introduced.

The instructions for running the program can easily be followed since all options are menu driven and use prompts.

TIPS AND TECHNIQUES

- Lines 20–60 present the study options that are available.

- Line 70 prompts the user to enter the option desired.

- Line 80: This line checks to see if a number greater than 5 is selected. If so, the user is reminded to select only values from 1 to 5; the program jumps back to line 70 to once again offer options 1 through 5. This technique is used to trap for an inappropriate response.

- Line 90: This line causes the program to branch to the selected module. If N = 1 then the program goes to line 200; if N = 2 the program goes to line 300; and if N = 5 the program goes to line 800. The first four modules have a similar structure—to be examined briefly.

- Lines 200–280 comprise the addition problem generator.

- Line 200 clears the screen and clears all variables so each time a new module is chosen the counters are reset to 0.

- Line 210 sends the program to a subroutine beginning at line 700 in which the user is prompted for the highest number desired.

- In line 710 the user is asked for the number of problems desired. The RETURN instruction ends the subroutine and brings the program back to line 220.

- Line 220 sends the program to another subroutine beginning at line 720. The subroutine at line 720 generates two random numbers, X and Y. The built in RND(X) function generates a random number in the range of 0–1. In the expression for generating X, the resultant number gets multiplied by the upper limit H. The integer value of the results is obtained by using the INT function. And finally, 1 is added to the result to insure that a number between 1 and the chosen upper limit is obtained. A similar approach is used to obtain a value for Y.

- Line 230 prints an addition expression using the values of X and Y.

- Line 240: This line prompts the user for the answer. The answer is assigned to variable A. The actual computed answer is assigned to variable Z.

- Line 250 looks for a match between A and Z. If they match, the reponse entered is correct. The correct answer counter, C is incremented; the problem counter, P is incremented. The program then branches to line 270.

- Line 260: If the answer is incorrect the screen displays the correct answer and the problem counter is incremented.

- Line 270 decides if the desired number of questions has been asked. (Remember the variable R, from line 710?) Variable R is matched against the problem counter P. If they match it means that all questions have been asked, and the number of correct answers is displayed. The program then branches to another subroutine at line 740. This subroutine asks the user if more questions are desired. If the answer is yes, the screen displays the program options again. If the answer is no, the program ends by executing the END statement at line 270.

- Line 280: If all the questions have not been answered, the program branches back to line 220 and generates the next question.

- Line 330 generates the subtraction equation.

- Lines 400–480 generate the multiplication problems, again following the same logic used in the first module.

- Lines 500–610: These lines generate the division problems. A difficulty faced when dealing with division questions is if the numerator and the denominator are not integer values, the answer may consist of a fractional part with many digits. In order to insure whole number quotients, the program deals with this possibility in line 550.

- Lines 550–570 break the solution into a quotient part Q, and into a remainder part D.

- Line 550: Variable Z is the integer part of the quotient X/Z. Variable M is the remainder part.

- Line 580: Only if the integer part and the remainder part are correct, is the answer considered correct.

- Lines 800–860 generate the multiplication table.

- Line 820 starts a loop where factors of the table start at 1 through 10.

- Line 830:D is the result of the multiplication.

- Line 860 branches to subroutine 740.

VARIABLES USED:

A: Your answer.
C: Correct answer counter.
D: Remainder of division module.
H: Highest number desired in study module.
M: Multiplier value.
N: Study option number.
P: Problem counter.
Q: Quotient in division module.
R: Number of problems to study.
X: First variable in generated problem.
Y: Second variable in generated problem.
Z: Integer value in division module, also actual computed answer.

PROGRAM LISTING

```
PRINT CHR$(147),"MATH TEACHER"
PRINT"OPTION #1 ADDITION"
PRINT"OPTION #2 SUBTRACTION"
PRINT"OPTION #3 MULTIPLICATION"
PRINT"OPTION #4 DIVISION"
PRINT"OPTION #5 MULTIPLICATION TABLES"
PRINT:PRINT:INPUT"PICK YOUR STUDY OPTION #";N
IF N>5 THEN PRINT"PICK #(1-5) ONLY":GOTO 70
ON N GOTO 200,300,400,500,800
0 PRINT CHR$(147),"ADDITION PRACTICE":CLR
0 GOSUB 700
0 GOSUB 720
0 PRINT:PRINT X;"+";Y;"=?":PRINT
0 INPUT"YOUR ANSWER=";A:Z=X+Y
0 IF A=Z THEN PRINT"CORRECT":C=C+1:P=P+1:GOTO 270
0 PRINT"WRONG-THE CORRECT ANSWER=";Z:P=P+1
0 IF R=P THEN PRINT"YOU GOT ";C;" OUT OF ";R:GOSUB 740:END
0 GOTO 220
0 PRINT CHR$(147),"SUBTRACTION PRACTICE":CLR
0 GOSUB 700
0 GOSUB 720
0 PRINT:PRINTX;"-";Y;"=?":PRINT
0 INPUT"YOUR ANSWER=";A:Z=X-Y
0 IF A=Z THEN PRINT"CORRECT":C=C+1:P=P+1:GOTO 370
0 PRINT"WRONG-THE CORRECT ANSWER=";Z:P=P+1
0 IF R=P THEN PRINT"YOU GOT ";C;" OUT OF ";R:GOSUB 740:END
0 GOTO 320
0 PRINT CHR$(147),"MULTIPLICATION PRACTICE":CLR
0 GOSUB 700
0 GOSUB 720
0 PRINT:PRINT X;"*";Y;"=?":PRINT
0 INPUT"YOUR ANSWER=";A:Z=X*Y
0 IF A=Z THEN PRINT"CORRECT":C=C+1:P=P+1:GOTO 470
0 PRINT"WRONG-THE CORRECT ANSWER=";Z:P=P+1
0 IF R=P THEN PRINT"YOU GOT ";C;" OUT OF ";R:GOSUB 740:END
0 GOTO 420
0 PRINT CHR$(147),"DIVISION PRACTICE":CLR
0 GOSUB 700
0 GOSUB 720
5 IF X<Y THEN GOTO 520
0 PRINT:PRINT X;"/";Y;"=?":PRINT
0 PRINT"ENTER THE QUOTIENT(WHOLE NUMBER RESULT) AND THE REMAINDER"
0 Z=INT(X/Y):M=X-Z*Y
0 PRINT:INPUT"QUOTIENT=";Q
0 PRINT:INPUT"REMAINDER=";D
0 IF Q=Z AND D=M THEN PRINT"CORRECT":C=C+1:P=P+1:GOTO 600
0 PRINT"WRONG-THE QUOTIENT=";Z:PRINT"REMAINDER=";M:P=P+1
0 IF R=P THEN PRINT"YOU GOT ";C;" OUT OF ";R:GOSUB 740:END
0 GOTO 520
0 INPUT"HIGHEST NUMBER TO STUDY=";H
0 INPUT"HOW MANY PROBLEMS DO YOU WANT";R:RETURN
0 X=INT(H*RND(1))+1:Y=INT(H*RND(1))+1
0 RETURN
0 PRINT:INPUT"WANT TO STUDY MORE(Y/N)";A$
0 IF A$="Y" THEN GOTO 10
0 PRINT:PRINT"HAVE A NICE DAY"
0 RETURN
```

```
800 PRINT CHR$(147),"MULTIPLICATION TABLES":CLR
810 INPUT"MULTIPLIER TO STUDY";M
820 FOR T=1 TO 10
830 D=T*M
840 PRINT T;" * "M;" =";D:PRINT
850 NEXT T
860 GOSUB 740
```

8. Loan Payment Primer

Occasionally you may find it necessary to borrow money. "Paying Loans" can help you analyze and calculate the factors involved in obtaining a bank loan. You will be able to calculate the most economical way to borrow money. Questions facing you might be: Can I move out of the city and buy a house in the suburbs at these high interest rates? Can I buy a new car? If so what will my monthly payment be?

This program offers three options with these features: Option #1 Computes the payment to be made on a loan. For example, you just bought a new car. What will the monthly payments be if you wish to pay off a loan of $8000 in 36 months? The interest rate is 13% annually.

Option #2: Computes the principal on a loan. For example you are willing to pay only $100 per month for 36 months for a used car. The annual interest rate is 13%. What is the principal that you must borrow?

Option #3: Computes the number of pay periods. For example: How many monthly payments of $150 will have to be made to pay off a loan of $4000 at the annual interest rate of 15%.

All options use prompts and are easy to follow.

One caution must be observed. When performing financial calculations all the parameters must be in the same time units. If you are trying to find the monthly payments on a loan made at an annual interest rate of 18%, "I" must be represented as the monthly interest rate or as 18%/12 or 1.5%.

This program illustrates the use of subroutines for text prompts used in many parts of the program. The program also introduces a routine for rounding off numbers to two decimal places.

TIPS AND TECHNIQUES

- Line 10 clears the screen.

- Lines 30–100 display the 3 available options.

- Line 120 prompts the user to select an option number.

- Line 130 checks if the user entered an option number that is illegal. If the number is greater than 3, the program branches back to line 120.

- Line 140 is a computed GOTO instruction. If the user selects option #1, then W = 1 and the program branches to line 200. If W = 2 it branches to line 300 and if W = 3 the program branches to line 400.

- Line 150: This FOR-NEXT loop displays four blank lines on the screen. It is used to format the display more attractively.

- Line 160 asks the user if any more calculations are desired.

- Line 170: If the answer is a "Y" for "YES", the program branches to line 10 and displays the available options again.

- Line 180: If the answer is "NO" the program ends at this line. It is important to include the "END" statement here, since the following lines of code include subroutines which would start executing without having been instructed to do so.

- Lines 200–280 compute the solution to option #1.

- Line 240 sends the program to a subroutine beginning at line 630. This line, which calculates the interest as a percentage, multiplies your input by .01.

- Line 250 sends the program to a subroutine at line 640 which performs the calculations involved in computing the principal.

- Line 270 performs the calculations in rounding off the answer. This is done by a call to a subroutine at line 900.

- Lines 300–380 perform the calculations required for option #2.

- Lines 400–480 perform the calculations required for option # 3.

- Lines 600–640 make up a short subroutine which prompts the user to input data parameters and performs the required calculations.

- Lines 900–930 comprise a subroutine which rounds off the calculations to two decimal places.

- Line 900: Variable A separates the integer part of the number. Variable B is the fractional part of the calculation.

- Line 910 rounds off the fractional part to two places. This is used to represent the cents part of the answer.

- Line 920 arrives at the final answer by adding the integer part and the rounded off fractional part.

VARIABLES USED:

A$ User's reply.
D: Final calculated answer.
I: Interest value.
D: Dummy variable to hold answers
M: Payment value.
N: Number of pay periods.
Q: Equation value.
R: Principal value.
W: Option number.
Z: Blank line index.

PROGRAM LISTING

```
10 PRINT CHR$(147):PRINT
20 PRINT TAB(15)"PAYING LOANS":PRINT
30 PRINT "OPTION 1"
40 PRINT"COMPUTE PAYMENT TO BE MADE"
50 PRINT
60 PRINT"OPTION 2"
70 PRINT"COMPUTE PRINCIPAL ON A LOAN"
80 PRINT
90 PRINT"OPTION 3"
100 PRINT"COMPUTE NUMBER OF PAY PERIODS"
110 PRINT:PRINT
120 INPUT"SELECT YOUR OPTION (1-3)";W
130 IF W>3 THEN PRINT"ENTER OPTION #(1-3)":GOTO 120
140 ON W GOTO 200,300,400
150 FOR Z=1 TO 4:PRINT:NEXT Z
160 INPUT"ANY MORE CALCULATIONS (Y/N)";A$
170 IF A$="Y" THEN GOTO 10
180 END
200 PRINT CHR$(147):PRINT
210 PRINT"COMPUTE THE PAYMENT TO BE MADE":PRINT
220 GOSUB 600
230 GOSUB 620
240 GOSUB 630
250 GOSUB 640
260 M=R*Q
270 K=M:GOSUB 900:M=D
280 PRINT:PRINT"PAYMENT=$";M:PRINT
290 GOTO 150
300 PRINT CHR$(147):PRINT
310 PRINT"COMPUTE PRINCIPAL ON A LOAN":PRINT
320 GOSUB 610
330 GOSUB 620
340 GOSUB 630
```

```
350 GOSUB 640:Q=1/Q
360 R=M*Q
370 K=R:GOSUB 900:R=D
380 PRINT:PRINT"PRINCIPAL=$";R
390 GOTO 150
400 PRINT CHR$(147):PRINT
410 PRINT"COMPUTE THE NUMBER OF PAY PERIODS":PRINT
420 GOSUB 600
430 GOSUB 610
440 GOSUB 630
450 N=-LOG(1-I*R/M)/LOG(1+I)
460 K=N:GOSUB 900:N=D
470 PRINT:PRINT"# OF PAY PERIODS=";N
480 PRINT"(UNITS ARE CONSISTENT WITH INTEREST RATE TIME UNITS)"
490 GOTO 150
600 INPUT"PRINCIPAL=$";R:RETURN
610 INPUT"PAYMENT=$";M:RETURN
620 INPUT"# OF PAY PERIODS=";N:RETURN
630 INPUT"INTEREST %=";I:I=.01*I:RETURN
640 Q=I/(1-(1+I)↑-N):RETURN
900 A=INT(K):B=K-A
910 C=INT(B*100+.5)/100
920 D=A+C
930 RETURN
```

9. Studying State Capitals

Can you identify the capital of Washington? How about that of North Dakota? No? Well, this program will help you study and review the capitals of each of the fifty states.

The program consists of two modules. In part one you have the opportunity to study the capitals. The name of the state is briefly displayed on the screen along with its capital. The screen then clears and a new state and capital are displayed. All fifty states are covered in this manner. If you feel that the display is on for too long or too short a period of time, the Tips and Techniques part of this chapter will show you how to alter the length of time for each display. After you have studied the capitals and are confident of your knowledge, you are ready for option number two which is the test mode. In the test mode a state is displayed, and you must provide the name of its capital. If your response is incorrect, you will be informed and the correct answer will be indicated. If your response is correct, it will be duly recognized. After each question you have the choice of continuing with the test or stopping. If you decide to stop, your score will be displayed—the number of correct responses out of the number of questions presented. Now, see if you can get fifty out of fifty.

TIPS AND TECHNIQUES

An important technique used in this program is the use of two arrays to store fifty elements each. One array is used to store the states' names, and the second stores those of the capitals. In the study mode the corresponding elements of each array are displayed. In the test mode the input response is checked against the corresponding capital array element. Now, on to see how it's done:

- Line 10: The "DIM" dimension statement instructs the computer to set aside room for fifty array elements for array S$, which stores the states' names. Room is set aside for the fifty elements to be stored in array C$, which stores the capitals' names. Notice that since you are dealing with alphabetic variables, as opposed to numerical values, you must use the string variable notation—the "$" symbol.

- Line 60 asks which mode the user desires. The program looks for a reply, which should be either the number 1 or 2. Variable A stores the choice.

- Line 70 checks for an inappropriate response. If the reply is greater than 2, you are informed that you have made an error and you are sent back to line 60 to reselect a 1 or 2. This technique is called "error trapping." If the user enters an inappropriate response to a question—in this case anything other than the digits 1 and 2—the program returns to the question to await an acceptable response.

- Line 80: The "ON A GOTO" statement branches to the correct segment of the program, depending on the value of variable A. If A equals 1 the program goes to line 200; if A equals 2 it goes to line 400.

- Lines 200–270 comprise the study mode section.

- Line 220 starts a loop for reading fifty pieces of data.

- Line 230: In this line the data is read into the array list. This data is composed of the array elements in array S$(N), the states; and in array C$(N), the capitals. Notice that when N = 1 we read S$(1) and C$(1), the first elements in each array.

- Lines 240–250: The indexed elements are displayed on the screen.

- Line 260: This is the display time delay loop. The computer "counts" from 1 to 3000 before displaying the next state and capital. If you wish the delay to be longer you can have the computer count from 1 to 5000. If you wish the delay to be shorter you can have the computer count from 1 to 500. You can adjust the delay to your own preference by changing the upper limit of the count.

- Line 270: The value of "N" is incremented and the loop permits you to read the next element into each array (back at line 230).

- Lines 280–290 prompt the user for a response to a question. If you wish to be tested you have to type a "Y" for yes, and if you don't wish to be tested you have to type an "N" for no.

- Line 300 accepts the reply as a string variable.

- Line 310: If the response is a "Y" the program goes to line 400 to start the test module.

- Line 320: If the reply is an "N" (for no) the program goes back to line 200 and repeats the study mode.

- Line 400 clears the screen for the test mode.

- Line 420 resets the correct answer counter, C, to zero and the wrong answer counter, W, to zero.

- Line 430 sets up a loop to read all the elements of the states and capitals into the respective arrays.

- Line 450 prints the name of a state.

- Line 460 asks for the name of the matching capital, Q$.

- Line 470 checks to see if the reply matches the stored value of C$(A). If the answer does not match, the correct answer is displayed and the wrong answer counter, W, is incremented. The program then branches to line 490. Notice the use of multiple statements on one line. It is advisable to try to group all related statements on one line.

- Line 480: If the reply is correct you are so informed; the correct answer counter, C, is incremented.

- Line 490 accepts a response from the user as to whether he wishes to continue.

- Line 500: If the reply is an "N," for no, the program goes to line 520.

- Line 510: If the reply is "Y," for yes, the program comes to this line and increments the loop for the next question.

- Line 520: If you choose not to continue, this line computes the total number of questions that were answered as variable T.

- Line 530 prints the number of correct answers given.

- Line 540: The end of the program. Notice the "END" statement. It keeps the program from running into the data elements.

- Lines 600–780 are the data statements consisting of the names of states and capitals. They are read as pairs of elements in line 230 and in line 440. You have to be careful when entering data elements. They must be entered exactly in the order they will be read (or they must be read in the arrangement they are entered). Any deviation will cause an erroneous readout of the array of elements.

VARIABLES USED:

A: Mode selection (line 60), also element counter (line 430).
C: Correct answer counter.
D: Delay loop counter.
N: Element counter (line 220).
T: Total number of questions.
W: Wrong answer counter.
A$: Test mode reply.
C$: Capital array.
Q$: Capital reply.
S$: State array.

PROGRAM LISTING

```
10 DIM S$(50),C$(50)
20 PRINT CHR$(147)
30 PRINT:PRINT TAB(15)"STATE CAPITALS"
40 PRINT:PRINT"MODE #1 STUDY CAPITALS":PRINT
50 PRINT"MODE #2 TEST":PRINT
60 INPUT"WHICH MODE DO YOU SELECT (TYPE 1 OR 2)";A
70 IF A>2 THEN PRINT"ERROR-TRY AGAIN":GOTO 60
80 ON A GOTO 200,400
200 PRINT CHR$(147):PRINT
210 PRINT"STUDY MODE":PRINT:PRINT
220 FOR N=1 TO 50
230 READ S$(N),C$(N)
240 PRINT"STATE:     ";S$(N):PRINT
250 PRINT"CAPITAL: ";C$(N):PRINT:PRINT:PRINT
260 FOR D=1 TO 3000:NEXT D
270 NEXT N
280 PRINT"ARE YOU READY TO BE TESTED (Y/N)? "
290 PRINT"(OTHERWISE STUDY MODE WILL BE REPEATED"
300 INPUT A$
310 IF A$="Y" THEN GOTO 400
320 GOTO 200
400 PRINT CHR$(147):PRINT
410 PRINT"STATE CAPITALS TEST":PRINT
420 C=0:W=0:RESTORE
430 FOR A=1 TO 50
440 READ S$(A),C$(A)
450 PRINT"STATE: ";S$(A):PRINT
460 INPUT"CAPITAL: ";Q$:PRINT
470 IF Q$<>C$(A) THEN PRINT"WRONG-CAPITAL IS ";C$(A):W=W+1:
        GOTO 490
480 C=C+1:PRINT"CORRECT!":PRINT
490 PRINT:INPUT"CONTINUE (Y/N)";B$:PRINT
500 IF B$="N" THEN GOTO 520
510 NEXT A
520 T=W+C
530 PRINT"YOU GOT ";C;" STATES OUT OF ";T
540 END
600 DATA ALABAMA,MONTGOMERY,ALASKA,JUNEAU,ARIZONA,PHOENIX
610 DATA ARKANSAS,LITTLE ROCK,CALIFORNIA,SACRAMENTO
```

```
615 DATA COLORADO,DENVER
620 DATA CONNECTICUT,HARTFORD,DELAWARE,DOVER
630 DATA FLORIDA,TALLAHASSEE,GEORGIA,ATLANTA
640 DATA HAWAII,HONOLULU,IDAHO,BOISE
650 DATA ILLINOIS,SPRINGFIELD,INDIANA,INDIANAPOLIS
655 DATA IOWA,DES MOINES
660 DATA KANSAS,TOPEKA,KENTUCKY,FRANKFORT,LOUISIANA,BATON ROUGE
670 DATA MAINE,AUGUSTA,MARYLAND,ANNAPOLIS,MASSACHUSETTS,BOSTON
680 DATA MICHIGAN,LANSING,MINNESOTA,ST. PAUL,MISSISSIPPI,JACKSON
690 DATA MISSOURI,JEFFERSON CITY,MONTANA,HELENA,NEBRASKA,LINCOLN
700 DATA NEVADA,CARSON CITY,NEW HAMPSHIRE,CONCORD
705 DATA NEW JERSEY,TRENTON
710 DATA NEW MEXICO,SANTA FE,NEW YORK,ALBANY
720 DATA NORTH CAROLINA,RALEIGH,NORTH DAKOTA,BISMARCK
725 DATA OHIO,COLUMBUS
730 DATA OKLAHOMA,OKLAHOMA CITY,OREGON,SALEM
740 DATA PENNSYLVANIA,HARRISBURG,RHODE ISLAND,PROVIDENCE
750 DATA SOUTH CAROLINA,COLUMBIA,SOUTH DAKOTA,PIERRE
755 DATA TENNESSEE,NASHVILLE
760 DATA TEXAS,AUSTIN,UTAH,SALT LAKE CITY,VERMONT,MONTPELIER
770 DATA VIRGINIA,RICHMOND,WASHINGTON,OLYMPIA
775 DATA WEST VIRGINIA,CHARLESTON
780 DATA WISCONSIN,MADISON,WYOMING,CHEYENNE
```

10. File Cabinet

Illustrating how the disk system works, this program stores and displays a sequential data file. You may use the program to keep track of your book collection, stamp collection, stocks or any other data you may wish to organize and file. The program, as written, is designed to organize a personal library. The file is formatted to include the author's name, and the title of the book. The program is composed of two parts.

Part One, called the "DATA FILER PROGRAM" prompts the user to enter the data which will be stored on the disk. The file created is named "DATA FILER."

Part Two of the program, called "SEQ. DATA FILER READER", retrieves the data file that was created and sequentially displays the information on the screen. Another option offered permits you to search through the file for a specific author.

This program utilizes some of the features that are explained in the disk *User's Manual* and in the *Programmer's Reference Guide*, both of which are available from Commodore.

TIPS AND TECHNIQUES

Part I: Data Filer Program

- Line 10 prints "DATA FILER PART" on the screen.

- Line 20 sets up two arrays each of which can hold 100 elements. Array variable A$ stores the author's name and array variable B$ stores the title of the book.

- Line 40: This statement is essential when starting to use the disk drive. It is used to open up the "COMMAND CHANNEL." The command channel is channel #15. The device # for the disk is #8.

- Line 45 branches to a subroutine at line 500 which is used to read the error channel (more on this later).

- Line 50 defines the variable CR$ as the code for RETURN or carriage return. It uses the predefined ASCII code for the RETURN function which is 13.

- Line 60 opens a file using the number of the file. In our case it is file #2. The file name is "DATA FILER." The S denotes that it is sequential and the W denotes that we are going to write data to that file. The notation @0: preceding the file name is a message to the disk operating system to replace any existing program using the indicated name with the new program. If you don't want your old program to be deleted use a different name for the new file.

- Line 65 branches to the error checking subroutine.

- Line 70 prompts the user to enter the author's name, a comma and then the title of the book.

- Line 80: If you wish to stop entering data the program instructs the user to type "QUIT."

- Line 90 prompts the user to enter the author's name.

- Line 95 checks to see if the input string matches the word "QUIT." If so the program branches to line 150 and stops the input process.

- Line 100 permits the user to enter the title of the book.

- Line 130 The PRINT # statement instructs the computer to write the data onto the disk. Notice the carriage return after each set of data is entered.

- Line 135 branches to the error checking routine.

- Line 140: If no error exists the program branches back to line 90 to permit the entry of more data.

- Line 150 closes the disk file. Every file that has been opened must be closed when you have finished entering data. If a file is not closed the data will be lost.

- Lines 500–550 consist of a subroutine which reads the error channel. The disk operating system can detect many operational and syntax errors. For more information on the error codes, refer to the disk manual. Your 64 computer does not inform you as to the nature of the errors. You must use a short program to gain that information.

- Line 500: The INPUT # reads 4 variables which can inform you of the errors detected. EN denotes the error # (refer to the table in the disk manual) EM$ indicates the type of error, ET indicates the track number on the disk containing the error (not the movie character), and ES the sector number.

- Line 510: If the error number is zero no error exists and all is okay. The program returns to the line following the subroutine call.

- Line 520: If EN is not zero, it means that an error exists.

- Line 530 prints all the error parameters.

- Line 540: Don't forget to close your file, especially if you don't wish to lose your data.

VARIABLES USED:

A$:   Author's name.
B$:   Title of the book.
EN: Error number.
EM$: Error description.
ES: Sector number.
ET: Track number.

PROGRAM LISTING

```
10 PRINT"DATA FILER PROGRAM"
20 DIM A$(100),B$(100)
40 OPEN 15,8,15
45 GOSUB 500
50 CR$=CHR$(13)
60 OPEN 2,8,2,"@0:DATA FILER,S,W"
65 GOSUB 500
70 PRINT:PRINT"ENTER NAME OF AUTHOR,COMMA,TITLE OF BOOK"
80 PRINT"ENTER 'QUIT' TO STOP"
90 INPUT"AUTHOR'S NAME:";A$
95 IF A$="QUIT" THEN 150
100 INPUT"TITLE:";B$
130 PRINT#2,A$","B$CR$
135 GOSUB 500
140 GOTO 90
150 CLOSE 2
160 END
500 INPUT#15,EN,EM$,ET,ES
510 IF EN=0 THEN RETURN
520 PRINT"DISK ERROR"
530 PRINT EN,EM$,ET,ES
540 CLOSE 2
550 END
```

Part II: Reading A Sequential Data File

This part of the program retrieves the data stored in Part I. The file contents are displayed in a scrolling fashion on the screen. An additional option permits you to search for a particular author in the file that you have created. This part of the program can be merged with Part I or it can remain a separate module and be used for other sequential data retrieval applications. Most of the code is similar to Part I. The error checking routine is the same as that in Part I.

• Line 210 opens the file. The file name is "DATA FILER."

• Line 220 sends the program to the error checking routine.

• Line 230: The "INPUT #" command is used to retrieve the data stored on the file. Notice that you define how the data variables are to be retrieved. Also notice that the comma separates each variable.

• Line 240 sets up a "STATUS" variable—more on this later.

• Line 250 checks for errors again.

• Lines 255–270 print on the screen the index number, the author and the title of the book.

• Line 280: This line is a delay loop used when displaying the information on the screen. If the display is scrolling too fast you can increase the upper limit of the loop to 1000.

• Line 290: If a "STATUS" value of 64 is detected then the disk operating system is instructed to close the file. The "STATUS (ST)" keyword is a system variable which detects conditions of INPUT/OUTPUT operation. If a code of 64 is detected it is recognized as an "END OF FILE."

• Line 300: If ST is not 64 but equals zero than a bad disk status has been detected.

• Lines 310–320 increment the index I, and retrieve the next piece of data from the disk.

• Lines 400–420: If a bad disk status has been detected the file is closed and the program ends.

• Lines 500–550 consist of the error detection subroutine which is the same as the routine in Part I.

- Lines 600–700 consist of the search routine.

- Line 620 searches the A$(N) array for the author's name. If it is found, the author and title are printed.

- Line 630: If the author's name is not found in the file, "NOT FOUND" is printed and the program ends.

- Lines 670–690 ask if another search is desired.

VARIABLES USED:

A$(I): The array storing the author's name.
B(I): The index number.
B$(I): The array storing the title of the book.
D: Delay loop.
I: Index value.
N: Index value.
Q$: User's reply.
ST: Status value.

PROGRAM LISTING

```
200 PRINT"SEQ DATA FILER READER "
201 OPEN 15,8,15
210 OPEN 2,8,2,"0:DATA FILER,S,R"
220 GOSUB 500
230 INPUT#2,A$(I),B$(I),B(I)
240 RS=ST
250 GOSUB 500
255 PRINT"INDEX #:"I+1
260 PRINT"AUTHOR:";A$(I)
270 PRINT"TITLE:";B$(I)
280 PRINT:PRINT:FOR D= 1 TO 500:NEXT D
290 IF RS=64 THEN CLOSE 2:GOTO 600
300 IF RS<>0 THEN 400
310 I=I+1
320 GOTO 230
400 PRINT"BAD DISK STATUS  ";RS
410 CLOSE 2
420 END
500 INPUT#15,EN,EM$,ET,ES
510 IF EN=0 THEN RETURN
520 PRINT"DISK ERROR"
530 PRINT EN,EM$;ET;ES
540 CLOSE2
550 END
600 INPUT "SEARCH FOR AUTHOR:";N$
610 FOR N=1 TO 100
```

```
620 IF N$=A$(N) THEN PRINT A$(N):PRINT B$(N):GOTO 670
630 NEXT N
640 PRINT"NOT FOUND":GOTO 700
670 PRINT:PRINT"SEARCH FOR MORE INFO(Y/N)?"
680 INPUT"(Y/N)";Q$
690 IF Q$="Y" THEN GOTO 600
700 PRINT"REMOVE YOUR DISK"
```

COMMODORE 64 IN THE PLAYROOM

11. Swordmaster

Your Kingdom is being attacked by a raiding party of goblins. The Dark Master has given these creatures the gift of swordsmanship. The King has lost many a good man under the blades of these fell demons. You are the Kingdom's last hope. If you fail, the Kingdom will be pillaged.

PLAYING

There are two methods of controlling your swordsperson. The main listing provides for keyboard entry of command data. If you happen to own a suitable joystick, you may also use that method, by altering the main listing as shown in listing 2.

With either method, you have four possible moves: upward block, downward block, thrust, and dodge/retreat. With the keyboard as the controller, use the U, N, J, and H keys, respectively. When using the joystick controller, refer to figure 1.

Rules are thus: You must needs kill twain of yon approaching uglies per round. Each round, thine enemies doth increase in performance, though. This means that, by the 10th round, each of the baddies can take up to 6 hits each!

You, however, will lose the Kingdom if your total number of hits taken exceeds 20 + the round number; i.e., if you are hit 26 times by the fifth round, you have lost.

HELPFUL HINTS

Your "weak" move is changed after you are hit; after each new round; or if you remain in engarde position.

Due to the action of the keyboard buffer, up to 10 moves may be stored. This comes from hitting the keys too fast. Keep it slow, as though you were actually swinging a heavy sword.

PROGRAM HIGHLIGHTS

Lines 1 and 2 print a nice little introduction and, in an amazing bit of computer magic, misdirect the player while constructing the SPRITE graphics necessary to play the game.

Line 10 begins the work by setting the variable V to the starting address of the VIC (Video Interface Chip). DP is set to 150, the value (location) of the first of eight SPRITE data blocks. Next, two sprites are assigned colors. SPRITE 0 is used to display the player's move, and is colored white. SPRITE 1, the goblin SPRITE, is colored light grey.

Next, the random number generator is seeded. Then, in line 12, the computer jumps to line 600, in order to begin playing the intro theme music. Note that the SPRITES haven't been formed yet.

Lines 600–615 set up the SID chip (Sound Interface Device) to produce a trumpet-like sound. Lines 620–625 provide the two oscillators with note values, set up the duration of the note, then call the delay routine at lines 700–710. After the fanfare sounds, the computer returns to line 20 for some unfinished business. Here, the SPRITES are given data blocks to provide the five player positions and the three goblin positions. The shape data are contained in the DATA lines (1000 to 1380). The REMark statements in between the DATA lines describe each shape.

Line 148 turns on the sprite images. Line 149 generates the floor which the sprites will walk on. Line 150 updates the round counter whenever two enemies are killed. Line 156 gets a random number which determines the players weakest move; up block, down block, thrust, or dodge. If the enemy thrusts when you are in this position, he will score a hit. The number chosen here refers to one of the four data blocks for the player sprite.

Lines 160–171 determine the goblin's move. Line 165 also moves the goblin forward whenever he thrusts. Line 175 displays the goblin at the location held in CX. If the goblin sprite is too close to the player sprite, line 180 moves the goblin backwards.

If the player does not choose a movement, the sprite will remain in the "engarde" position. If the goblin thrusts during this time, line 181 causes the scoring of a hit against the player. Lines 185–210 decode the player input into sprite movement. Line 200 advances the player whenever "thrust" is chosen. Line 211 displays the sprite at the location held in PX.

Lines 215–217 determine which side scores a hit. Lines 222–224 determine when the two swords clash, and jump to the "clang" routine at 500–530. After this, the program jumps back to line 160.

Figure 1.

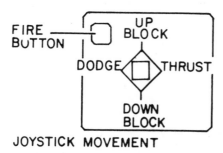

JOYSTICK MOVEMENT

PROGRAM LISTING

```
1 Printchr$(14);"█████████████████Sword master██":Print:Print
2 Print"████Your quest is to destroy the in-":Print" vading
     army and save the Kingdom."
10   v=53248:dP=150:Pokev+39,1:Pokev+40,15
11   w=rnd(-ti):w=0:rem *seed rnd gen.
12   gosub600
20   forx=dPto157:sd=x*64
25   rem dP=sprite data block:sd=actual memory loc. of dP
30   forbn=0to62:readd:Pokebn+sd,d:nextbn
40   next x:rem ***sprites done***
45   rem *set up initial sprite x,y
50   Pokev,100:Pokev+1,100:rem        s0
60   Pokev+2,150:Pokev+3,100:rem      s1
125  rem *now assign initial data blocks
130  Poke2040,150:Poke2041,155
145  rem *now get into main prgm
146  ed=0:rn=1:Print"█"
148  Pokev+21,3:Px=110:cx=160:Pokev,Px:Pokev+2,cx
149  forfl=1384to1423:Pokefl,160:Pokefl+54272,7:
        next:w=Peek(v+30)
150  Print"█████████*******READY":ed=ed+1:ifed=2thened=0:goto153
151  goto154
153  rn=rn+1:gosub600:rem round counter
154  Print"████████████████Round:██ ";rn:ep=int((rnd(0)*3)+1)+15
155  ifrn=11thenPrint"███████████Final Round██"
156  Pw=int((rnd(0)*4)+1)+150
160  cP=int(rnd(0)*6)+1:ifcP=1thencP=155
165  ifcP=2thencP=156:cx=cx-2
170  ifcP=3thencP=157
171  if(cP>3)and(cP<7)thencP=157
175  Poke2041,cP:Pokev+2,cx
180  ifcx<(Px+10)thencx=cx+10
181  if(cP=156)and(Peek(2040)=150)and(cx<Px+11)then260
185  getPi$:Poke2040,150:ifPi$=""then155
190  ifPi$="u"thenPP=151
195  ifPi$="n"thenPP=152
200  ifPi$="j"thenPP=153:Px=Px+2
210  ifPi$="h"thenPP=154:Px=Px-10
211  Poke2040,PP:Pokev,Px
215  if(PP=153)and(cP=ep)and(Peek(v+30)=3)then230
217  if(cP=156)and(PP=Pw)and(Peek(v+30)=3)then260
218  ifPx<30thenPx=30
219  ifcx>190thencx=190
220  ifPx>190thenPx=185
221  ifcx<30thencx=40
222  if(PP=151)and(cP=155)thengosub500
223  if(PP=152)and(cP=157)thengosub500
224  if(PP=153)and(cP=156)thengosub500
225  goto160
230  se=se+1:Print"██████████Hits to Enemy:     ████";se;"█"
231  ifse<1+(rn/2)then160
```

```
135 ifrn>10then310
140 se=0:P3=P3+1:Print"............Enemies: ";P3
150 Pokev+21,1:forzc=1to1500:nextzc:Print"":goto148
160 P2=P2+1:Print"..............Hits: ";P2:forzc=1to1500:
    next
170 ifP2>rn+20then290
180 goto 155
190 Pokev+21,2:Print"..................The  Victor.."
200 end
210 Pokev+21,1:Print"..................The  Victor.."
220 Print"      RATING       ":Print:Print"    ";
230 ifP2<8thenPrint"Swordmaster":goto400
231 ifP2<11thenPrint"Knight":goto450
232 ifP2<14thenPrint"Swordsman":end
233 ifP2<17thenPrint"Warrior":end
234 ifP2<20thenPrint"Fighter":end
235 ifP2<24thenPrint"Brigand":end
236 ifP2>23thenPrint"Peasant-in-training":end
237 end
400 forPk=150to153:gosub501:Poke2040,Pk:forPl=1to400:nextPl:nextPk
410 gosub600:Print"":Pokev+21,0:end
450 forPk=151to152:gosub501:Poke2040,Pk:forPl=1to800:nextPl:nextPk
460 gosub600:Print"":Pokev+21,0:end
500 ifPeek(v+30)<>3thenreturn
501 Poke54296,15:Poke54277,0:Poke54278,231
505 Poke54284,0:Poke54285,231
510 Poke54273,155:Poke54272,120
515 Poke54280,int(rnd(0)*2)+105:Poke54279,int(rnd(0)*255)+1
520 Poke54276,33:Poke54283,21:forz3=1to49:next
525 Poke54276,32:Poke54283,20
530 return
590 rem***subroutine to play main theme***
600 Poke54296,15:Poke54277,21:Poke54278,199
605 Poke54284,21:Poke54285,199:Poke54276,33:Poke54283,33
620 Poke54273,17:Poke54272,37:Poke54280,45:Poke54279,198:lv=100:
    gosub700
621 Poke54273,17:Poke54272,37:Poke54280,45:Poke54279,198:lv=150:
    gosub700
622 Poke54273,22:Poke54272,227:Poke54280,61:Poke54279,126:lv=300:
    gosub700
624 Poke54273,17:Poke54272,37:Poke54280,45:Poke54279,198:lv=100:
    gosub700
625 Poke54273,22:Poke54272,227:Poke54280,61:Poke54279,126:lv=590:
    gosub700
626 Poke54276,32:Poke54283,32:return
700 fortd=1tolv:next:Poke54276,32:Poke54283,32
710 Poke54276,33:Poke54283,33:return
800 rem *****64 engarde*****
810 data 12,0,0,30,0,0,63,0,0,30,0,0,12,0,0,255,194,0,255,242
815 data 0,223,127,254,223,63,255,223,2,0,223
820 data 2,0,31,0,0,63,128,0,123,192,0,241,224,0,224
830 data 224,0,113,192,0,113,192,0,59,128,0,31,0,0,127,192,0
840 rem *****64 up block*****
850 data 6,0,0,15,0,12,31,128,28,15,0,56,6,0,112,31,196,224
860 data 127,227,192,239,179,128,207,159,128,207,156,64,207
```

```
1070 data 136,0,207,128,0,31,192,0,61,224,0,120,240,0,96,48
1080 data 0,112,112,0,56,224,0,24,192,0,24,192,0,120,240,0
1090 rem *****64 down block*****
1100 data 3,0,0,7,128,0,15,192,0,231,128,0,243,0,0,223,128,0
1110 data 207,240,0,207,248,0,207,140,0,15,140,128,15,135
1120 data 0,15,131,0,31,199,128,61,233,192,120,240,224,96,48
1130 data 112,112,112,56,56,224,28,24,192,14,24,192,2,120,240,
1140 rem *****64 thrust*****
1150 data 0,0,0,0,96,0,0,240,0,1,248,0,0,240,0,0,96,0,7,248
1160 data 0,15,248,0,25,234,0,49,234,0,35,239,254,39,239,255
1170 data 7,194,0,15,130,0,13,192,0,28,224,0,56,96,0
1180 data 112,192,0,96,192,0,193,128,0,112,224,0
1190 rem *****64 dodge*****
1200 data 0,0,0,0,96,0,0,240,0,1,248,0,0,240,0,0,48,0,3
1210 data 255,208,14,126,56,24,61,16,48,56,224,24,19,192
1220 data 12,6,32,4,12,192,0,25,224,0,50,112,0,100,48,0
1230 data 200,24,1,144,24,1,56,28,2,24,12,0,112,15
1240 rem *****evil engarde*****
1250 data 64,27,96,64,39,144,96,15,192,96,7,128,48,3,0,56
1260 data 31,224,28,63,240,14,167,248,7,103,220,3,231
1270 data 196,4,199,196,0,135,196,0,7,196,0,14,224,0,28,112
1280 data 0,24,48,0,24,48,0,24,48,0,24,48,0,24,48,0,120,240
1290 rem *****evil thrust*****
1300 data 0,53,128,0,78,64,0,31,0,0,14,0,0,6,0,0,31,0,0,63
1310 data 128,0,63,192,1,46,192,129,47,96,127,175,176,63
1320 data 239,152,1,15,200,1,15,200,0,29,224,0,56,96,0,28
1330 data 112,0,28,56,0,12,28,0,12,6,0,56,28
1340 rem *****evil down block*****
1350 data 0,27,96,0,39,144,0,15,192,0,7,128,0,3,0,0,63,224,0
1360 data 255,240,4,199,248,3,135,220,3,7,196,7,135,196,14,7,
     196,28,7,196
1370 data 56,14,224,240,28,112,96,24,48,0,24,48,0,24,48,0,24
1380 data48,0,24,48,0,120,240
```

JOYSTICK MOVEMENT

Listing 2—Joystick for Swordmaster

```
185 pi = Peek(56320):Poke2040, 150: ifpi = 127then155
190 ifpi = 126thenpp = 151
195 ifpi = 125thenpp = 152
200 ifpi = 119thenpp = 153:px = px + 2
210 ifpi = 123thenpp = 154:px = px - 10
```

12. Bug Run

In this program, you play the part of an industrious beetle, trying to bring home the bacon. Your present locale is the first floor of a very busy department store. Your home is on the tenth floor. For every foot forward, there's a foot above you...ready to step on top of you!

PLAYING

After RUNning the program, eight boots will appear on the screen. Your player marker is the solid white circle (SHIFT Q). Hit any key to make the symbol appear in the starting block. Then, to move, use the period "." key to move right and the comma "," key to move left.

To get to each succeeding level, you must get from the right side of the screen to the left, without getting squashed by one of the boots. The level number will be displayed, as you go.

If you are unfortunate, and are squashed, pressing any key will re-start the game.

PROGRAM HIGHLIGHTS

Line 5 clears the screen before calling the subroutine to set up the SID for the boot thump sounds. Line 10 turns on all eight sprites, initializes the screen address (SA) for the bug dot and resets the level counter (L). Line 25 sets all the sprite foreground colors to white. Line 30 POKEs in the sprite shape. Lines 40 and 50 set up the eight sprite initial X and Y coordinates. Line 60 assigns data block 150 to the eight sprites. Lines 70 to 80 place the sprites on the screen. Line 187 clears the line of the display on which the bug will travel.

The main routine in this program consists of seven parts. Lines 90 to 117 contain the programming which directs the flow for the seven routines.

The first routine is a subroutine, beginning at line 200. In line 200, a counter variable (CV) is incremented by the level number. If the total held in CV is less than five, this routine is bypassed. When the total is greater than five, DF is filled with a random number which will vary in range according to the level number of the game. At level 1, the number will be from 0 to 29. At level 9, the number will be between 0 and 21. This random number is used to determine which boot will stomp. If the number in DF is less than eight, one of the boots will be activated; if the number is eight or greater, no boot is chosen.

The end result is that the boots will be more active at higher playing levels.

The second routine is the player input routine, from lines 120 to 150. If no key has been depressed prior to the calling of this subroutine, it will be bypassed. However, if a key has been depressed, it will be stored in the keyboard buffer, until this point. This subroutine decodes the player's movement and displays the move. If the player has made it to the left of the screen, line 131 sets the flag (NS) to indicate the level has been completed.

The third routine (appearing on line 90) checks to see if the NS flag is set. If so, the program jumps to line 85 to update the level number. If NS is *not* set, the program drops to the next line to call the fourth routine.

The fourth routine begins at line 700. This routine first moves the appropriate boot from half way to its fully down position then calls the routine (900-930) which outputs the boot's thump. At line 708, the sprite-character collision register is read. If a sprite has made contact with a screen character, this register will hold the value of the sprite which collided with the data: i.e. this register detects when a boot has squashed your bug. When this is true, lines 600-630 output a message, then await a key depression to restart the game. If the bug is still safe, the RETURN is to line 109 for the fifth routine.

The fifth routine is a simple time delay. The FOR...NEXT loop may be deleted for a faster game. After the delay, the sixth routine is called, beginning at line 800. This simply lifts the boot up to the half-way point. The boot is fully retracted in the final routine, from lines 110-117. After that, the program jumps back to line 90 to begin the cycle again.

PROGRAM LISTING

```
5 CLR:PRINT"")":GOSUB1000
10 V=53248:POKEV+21,255:L=0:SA=1534:E1=PEEK(V+31)
25 FORTT=V+39TOV+46:POKETT,1:NEXT
30 FORP=0TO62:READD:POKE9600+P,D:NEXT
40 X0=30:X1=55:X2=90:X3=115:X4=150:X5=175:X6=210:X7=235
50 Y0=100:Y1=100:Y2=100:Y3=100:Y4=100:Y5=100:Y6=100:Y7=
60 FORCC=2040TO2047:POKECC,150:NEXT
70 POKEV,X0:POKEV+1,Y0:POKEV+2,X1:POKEV+3,Y1:POKEV+4,X2
   POKEV+5,Y2
75 POKEV+6,X3:POKEV+7,Y3:POKEV+8,X4:POKEV+9,Y4:
   POKEV+10,X5:POKEV+11,Y5
80 POKEV+12,X6:POKEV+13,Y6:POKEV+14,X7:POKEV+15,Y7
81 TI$="000000"
85 L=L+1:PRINT"        LEVEL:  ";L:NS=0
86 IFL>10THEN300
87 FORPP=1504TO1534:POKEPP,32:POKEPP+54272,1:NEXT
90 GOSUB200:GOSUB120:IFNS=1THEN85
```

```
109 GOSUB700:FORTT=1TO250:NEXT:GOSUB800
110 IFDF=0THENPOKEV+1,100
111 IFDF=1THENPOKEV+3,100
112 IFDF=2THENPOKEV+5,100
113 IFDF=3THENPOKEV+7,100
114 IFDF=4THENPOKEV+9,100
115 IFDF=5THENPOKEV+11,100
116 IFDF=6THENPOKEV+13,100
117 IFDF=7THENPOKEV+15,100
119 GOTO90
120 GETA$:IFA$=""THENRETURN
125 POKESA,81:POKESA+3,32:POKESA-3,32
130 IFA$=","THENSA=SA-3
131 IFSA=<1505THENSA=1534:NS=1:RETURN
135 IFA$="."THENSA=SA+3:IFSA>1534THENSA=1534
136 POKESA,81:POKESA+3,32:POKESA-3,32
150 RETURN
200 CV=CV+L:IFCV<5THENRETURN
201 CV=0
202 DF=INT(RND(0)*(30-L))
203 IFDF=0THENPOKEV+1,115
204 IFDF=1THENPOKEV+3,115
205 IFDF=2THENPOKEV+5,115
206 IFDF=3THENPOKEV+7,115
207 IFDF=4THENPOKEV+9,115
208 IFDF=5THENPOKEV+11,115
209 IFDF=6THENPOKEV+13,115
210 IFDF=7THENPOKEV+15,115
211 IFPEEK(V+31)<>0THENGOTO600
215 RETURN
300 PRINT"◌":ET$=TI$
310 PRINT:PRINT:PRINT:EH$=LEFT$(ET$,2):
      EM$=MID$(ET$,3,2):ES$=RIGHT$(ET$,2)
320 PRINT"    YOU'VE COMPLETED THE RUN IN:":PRINT
330 PRINTTAB(13);EH$;":";EM$;":";ES$
340 STOP
500 RETURN
600 POKESA,100:POKESD+1,2:POKESD,155:POKESD+4,33
605 POKEV+21,0:PRINT"◌YOU'VE BEEN SQUASHED!"
610 PRINT"LAST LEVEL COMPLETED:";L-1
615 POKESD+4,32:FORTT=1TO2500:NEXT
620 GETA$:IFA$=""THEN620
630 CLR:RUN
700 IFDF=0THENPOKEV+1,130:GOSUB900
701 IFDF=1THENPOKEV+3,130:GOSUB900
702 IFDF=2THENPOKEV+5,130:GOSUB900
703 IFDF=3THENPOKEV+7,130:GOSUB900
704 IFDF=4THENPOKEV+9,130:GOSUB900
705 IFDF=5THENPOKEV+11,130:GOSUB900
```

```
706  IFDF=6THENPOKEV+13,130:GOSUB900
707  IFDF=7THENPOKEV+15,130:GOSUB900
708  IFPEEK(V+31)<>0THENGOTO600
710  RETURN
800  IFDF=0THENPOKEV+1,115
801  IFDF=1THENPOKEV+3,115
802  IFDF=2THENPOKEV+5,115
803  IFDF=3THENPOKEV+7,115
804  IFDF=4THENPOKEV+9,115
805  IFDF=5THENPOKEV+11,115
806  IFDF=6THENPOKEV+13,115
807  IFDF=7THENPOKEV+15,115
810  RETURN
900  SD=54272:POKESD+4,129
910  FORSL=1TO150-(L*10):NEXT
920  POKESD+4,128
930  RETURN
1000 REM"BOOT SOUND ROUTINE"
1010 SD=54272:POKESD+24,15
1020 POKESD+5,0:POKESD+6,251
1030 POKESD+1,6:POKESD,6
1040 RETURN
9130 DATA 0,2,254,0,3,254,0,2,254
9140 DATA 0,3,254,0,2,254,0,3,254
9150 DATA 0,2,254,0,3,254,0,2,254
9160 DATA 0,3,250,0,5,250,0,15,250
9170 DATA 0,23,251,60,63,251,102,95,249
9180 DATA 123,255,253,127,255,253,255,255,253
9190 DATA 255,252,255,255,240,255,255,192,254
```

13. Arsonist!

You're the newly elected Fire Chief of Videoville; a quiet, quaint suburb of Game City. However, the ex-Fire Chief has suddenly gone crazy and wants to have you thrown out of office. He has hired a band of professional arsonists to burn down all of Videoville! Your job is to 1) put out the fires, and 2) catch the arsonists.

PLAYING

The structure of the game is such that you *must* put out as many fires as you can before apprehending the arsonist. Otherwise, you will lose points for every existing fire. If you wait too long, the arsonist will set too many fires, and you'll lose points anyway!

To move, use the "J" key to move right, the "H" key to move left, the "N" key to move down screen, and the "U" key to move up screen. You will score 5 points for every fire you put out, 100 points for capturing each arsonist. However, you will lose 5 points for every existing fire after nabbing the criminal.

PROGRAM HIGHLIGHTS

Lines 1, 2, 8, and data statements on lines 900–970 are used to program in a partial character set. Line 3 sets the background color. Lines 6 and 7 set the colors to be used in displaying the new multi-colored characters. Line 4 puts the 64 into the Multicolor Character Mode. Line 5 moves the character data address to allow the computer to get its characters from RAM, rather than from the ROM character generator. The new character generator is stored in memory, beginning at memory location (not to be confused with line number) 8192.

Lines 9–50 print information on the screen. When viewed in the standard character mode, the screen is filled with "@" and "A" characters. In the new character set, the "@" is the left side of a tiny house, the "A" is the right side. Since the listing is shown in the standard character format, it will seem a little strange. In lines 40 and 50, for instance, the string "BCDEFG" will be displayed on screen as "SCORE:", "BCEG" will appear as "SCR:". "SCR:" denotes the screen level at which you are playing. The numbers 0–9 will appear in their normal state, although in a different style of type. They appear larger, due in part to the multicolor mode, which uses a 4 by 8 dot matrix, whereas the standard character mode uses an 8 by 8 grid (although most of the characters utilize only a 5 by 7 portion).

Line 100 sets up variables which will be used later to move the player and arsonist characters. Line 105 places both characters in their respective starting locations. Line 110 replaces the player symbol with a space. Line 115 scans the keyboard for a player to move. If the player has depressed a key, the key is picked up by F$, then transferred to M$. Had no key been pressed, the program would have jumped to line 120.

Lines 120–150 will either update new movements, or else will maintain the last valid move. Each command will modify the position of the player in screen memory. Lines 120–150 also define the limits of movement within screen memory.

Line 160 looks into the screen memory block specified by the number in PL. If the block does not contain a code of 32 (space), the subroutine at line 270 will be called. More about this later.

Line 165 checks to see if the next block in screen memory is the arsonist character. If so, the player score is increased by 100. The enemy flag (EF) is then set. Line 170 puts the player back on screen, in the new location, and then checks the enemy flag variable. If EF is set, the program flow transfers to line 400 (after EF is reset).

Now, back to the subroutine at line 270. This is called only when the next move will cause the player to move into an occupied space. In this case, there must be one of three things in that block; the arsonist (checked at line 270), a segment of a house (which will either be burning or not), and a border or off-limit block.

If the block is a segment of a house which is burning, line 271 will recognize and put out the fire. If the block is neither an arsonist, nor a burning segment of a house, lines 275–300 adjust the position of the player to the nearest free space, based on the direction of travel.

After processing the player information, the computer begins to check movement and display the arsonist. This is done in a parallel fashion to that of the player. Of course, the arsonist detects non-burning house segments, and sets them on fire.

The computer determines the arsonist's movement in lines 190–230. This movement is generated by a rather rudimentary artificial intelligence method. Line 190 generates a random number between 1 and 8. If the number chosen is less than five, it is then tested (in lines 195–198) to determine whether it is a 1 or a 2. If the number is in fact a 1 or 2, no further tests are made upon it and the arsonist will either move up (on a 1) or down (on a 2). If the number was less than five, yet greater than two (i.e., a three or a four), then, again in lines 195–198, the movement is determined by checking the next block up, down, right and left. If any of these four blocks contain the player character (screen display code 8), the arsonist will move away from the player. If none of the four blocks checked contain the player, then the movement will be either to the right (on 3) or left (on a 4).

Back to line 190: If the random number was a five or greater, the direction will be chosen based on the nearest fire-setting route available. To understand this a little better, let's look more closely at lines 191 to 194.

Line 191 looks into the screen memory location which is two blocks above the arsonist. If this isn't a blank space, chances are it's a house. The direction variable (M) is set to 2, allowing the arsonist to move towards the house (which may actually be the player). Similarly, line 192 checks the block to the right. If this is an occupied location, the M setting is set to three, and the arsonist moves to the right. Line 193 checks the left; line 194 checks two blocks down.

Lines 200–230 process the M, or movement variable, checking also for out of bounds conditions.

PROGRAM LISTING

```
1 FORT=8448TO8455:POKET,0:NEXT
2 FORT=8192TO8271:READD:POKET,D:NEXTT
3 POKE53281,12
4 POKE53270,216
5 POKE53272,24
6 POKE53282,11
7 POKE53283,15
8 FORT=8576TO8655:READD:POKET,D:NEXT
9 PRINT"⬜"
10 PRINT"******************************************"
15 FORX=1TO5
20 PRINT"1⬜A      ⬜A ⬜A ⬜A ⬜A           ⬜A      ⬜A ⬜A1"
21 PRINT"1                                                1"
25 PRINT"1⬜A ⬜A ⬜A      ⬜A      ⬜A ⬜A      ⬜A ⬜A1"
26 PRINT"1                                                1"
30 NEXT
40 PRINT"⬛⬛⬛⬛⬛⬛⬛⬛DOOOOOOOOOOOOOOOOOOOOOOBCDEFG";PS
50 PRINT"⬜";TAB(25);"BCEG";1
90 L=12:SF=0
100 PP=32:EP=32:PC=8:EC=9:PL=1854:EL=1476:SF=0
105 POKEPL,PC:POKEEL,EC:FORGG=1TO1500:NEXT
110 POKEPL,PP
111 FORP9=1TO(L*17)-51:NEXT
115 GETF$:IFF$<>""THENM$=F$
120 IFM$="U"THENPL=PL-40:IFPL<1064THENPL=PL+40
130 IFM$="N"THENPL=PL+40:IFPL>1864THENPL=PL-40
140 IFM$="J"THENPL=PL+1:IFPL>1864THENPL=PL-1
150 IFM$="H"THENPL=PL-1:IFPL<1064THENPL=PL+1
160 PP=PEEK(PL):IFPP<>32THENGOSUB270
165 IFPP=9THENPS=PS+150:POKEEL,32:EF=1
170 POKEPL,PC:IFEF=1THENEF=0:GOTO400
175 IFPP=9THENPS=PS+100:POKEEL,32:EF=1
180 POKEEL,EP
190 F=INT(RND(0)*8)+1:IFF<5THENM=F:GOTO195
191 IFF>4THENIFPEEK(EL+80)<>32THENM=2
192 IFF>4THENIFPEEK(EL+1)<>32THENM=3
193 IFF>4THENIFPEEK(EL-1)<>32THENM=4
194 IFF>4THENIFPEEK(EL-80)<>32THENM=1
```

```
195 IFF>2THENIFPEEK(EL-40)=8THENM=2
196 IFF>2THENIFPEEK(EL-1)=8THENM=3
197 IFF>2THENIFPEEK(EL+1)=8THENM=4
198 IFF>2THENIFPEEK(EL+40)=8THENM=1
200 IFM=1THENEL=EL-40:IFEL<1064THENEL=EL+40
210 IFM=2THENEL=EL+40:IFEL>1864THENEL=EL-40
220 IFM=3THENEL=EL+1:IFEL>1864THENEL=EL-1
230 IFM=4THENEL=EL-1:IFEL<1064THENEL=EL+1
240 EP=PEEK(EL):IFEP<>32THENGOSUB340
250 POKEEL,EC
260 GOTO110
270 IFPP=9THENPS=PS+150+(10*(13-L)):POKEEL,32:EF=1
271 IF(PEEK(PL+54272)AND(14))<>14THENPOKEPL+54272,14:
        PS=PS+10+(13-L):SF=SF-1
272 PP=32
275 IFM$="J"THENPL=PL-1
280 IFM$="H"THENPL=PL+1
290 IFM$="U"THENPL=PL+40
300 IFM$="N"THENPL=PL-40
310 IFPP=9THENPS=PS+100:POKEEL,32:EF=1
320 PRINT"◆◆◆◆◆◆◆◆◆◆◆◆◆◆◆◆◆◆◆◆◆◆◆◆◆◆◆BCDEFG";PS
330 RETURN
340 IFEP=8THENPS=PS+100:POKEEL,32:EF=1
341 IF(PEEK(EL+54272)AND(15))<>2THENPOKEEL+54272,2:
        SF=SF+1:IFSF>50THEN400
342 EP=32
350 IFM=1THENEL=EL+40
360 IFM=2THENEL=EL-40
370 IFM=3THENEL=EL-1
380 IFM=4THENEL=EL+1
390 RETURN
400 US=PS-SF:POKE53281,1:POKE53280,0
410 FORTT=PSTOUSSTEP-1
415 PRINT"◆◆◆◆◆◆◆◆◆◆◆◆◆◆◆◆◆◆◆◆◆◆◆◆◆◆◆◆            "
420 PRINT"◆◆◆◆◆◆◆◆◆◆◆◆◆◆◆◆◆◆◆◆◆◆◆◆◆◆◆◆BCDEFG";TT
425 IFPS<0THEN460
426 NEXT:PS=US:POKE53281,12:POKE53280,12
427 PRINT"◆◆◆◆◆◆◆◆◆◆◆◆◆◆◆◆◆◆◆◆◆◆◆◆◆◆◆◆◆            "
428 PRINT"◆◆◆◆◆◆◆◆◆◆◆◆◆◆◆◆◆◆◆◆◆◆◆◆◆◆◆◆◆BCDEFG";PS
430 L=L-1:IFL<3THEN460
440 PRINT"⏎";TAB(25);"BCEG";(13-L)
450 POKEEL,32:POKEPL,32:GOTO100
460 POKE53281,1:GOTO470
465 POKE53281,INT(RND(0)*7)+7
470 FORTC=1TO2500
475 GETR$:IFR$="R"THENRUN
480 NEXT
490 GOTO465
900 DATA3,13,55,223,39,39,47,42,192,112,220,247,184,184,184,16
910 DATA84,84,64,84,84,4,84,84,20,84,64,64,64,64,84,20
915 DATA16,84,68,68,68,68,84,16
920 DATA80,84,68,68,80,84,68,68,20,84,64,80,80,64,84,20
930 DATA20,20,20,0,0,20,20,20
931 DATA20,20,85,170,170,85,20,20,192,192,192,192,255,255,255,
935 DATA84,68,68,68,68,68,68,84
940 DATA 4,4,4,4,4,4,4,4,84,84,4,84,84,64,84,84
950 DATA84,84,4,84,84,4,84,84,68,68,68,84,4,4,4,4,84,84,64,84
960 DATA4,4,4,84,84,64,64,84,68,68,68,84,84,4,4,4,4,4,4,4
970 DATA84,68,68,84,68,68,68,84,84,68,68,84,4,4,4,4
```

14. Music, Maestro

Note: This program is not a game. It has been devised in order for you to take advantage of the excellent sound synthesizer in the Commodore 64. It is heartily recommended that you read Chapter 7 in the Commodore 64 *User's Guide.* Also recommended is Chapter 4 in the *Programmer's Reference Guide.*

Using this program, you can compose music, translate written music into a form the computer can understand and, therefore, play; you are able to explore the many different sounds which the computer can generate.

For those of you who have no access to a copy of the *Programmer's Reference Guide*, and since the *User's Guide* explains nothing of the filter section of the SID chip, a brief description is in order.

There are three types of tone filters available; high pass, low pass, and band pass. By combining the high and low pass filters, a fourth filter may be emulated; this is known as band reject, or notch filter. The high pass filter does as its name implies; it allows high frequencies to pass through it, unaffected. The lower frequencies, or notes, are attenuated, or, to put it more simply, are cut down in volume. The low pass filter does the reverse; it allows the lower notes to pass, while attenuating the higher ones. You've used these filters before; they appear on most stereo units as the bass and treble controls; the low pass filter as the bass control, the high pass filter as the treble control.

The band-pass and band-reject filters are also aptly named. Both filters allow a certain cross section, or band, of frequencies to be modified. The band-pass filter attenuates the frequencies on either side of the band, allowing the middle range of frequencies to pass. This type of filter is found on some stereo units as the mid-range tone control.

The band-reject filter is just the opposite. In this filter, the band of frequencies is attenuated, allowing the frequencies on either side of the band to remain un-affected. This type of filter is most normally used to eliminate unwanted frequencies, such as the 60-Hz hum generated by an AC power line. If your stereo has a hum suppression circuit, it is most likely a band-reject filter.

For the three filters in the Commodore 64, two controls are provided; the cut-off frequency can be specified, as well as the resonance of the filter. The cut-off frequency determines the corner frequencies for high-or low-pass filters as well as the center frequencies for the band-pass filters. (See figure 1). This value, denoted by the symbol Fc, determines the final output of the sound. Changing the value is analogous to turning up or down a bass or treble control. Resonance effects are shown in figure 2. As the resonance value is increased, the slope of the filter (graphed as in figure 2) is sharpened. This simply means that the frequency at which maximum attenuation is exhibited is at higher resonance values, closer to the cut-off frequency than at lower resonance values.

Figure 1- Graphs of filter responses.

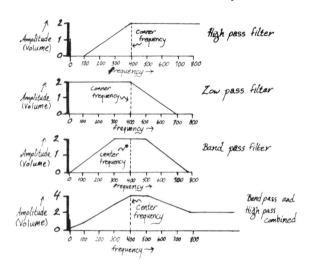

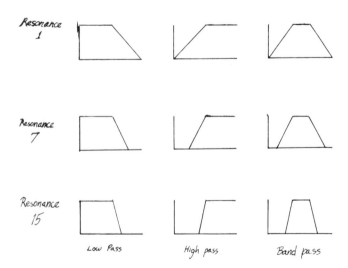

Figure 2 - Resonance effects

USING THE MUSIC PROGRAM

The first sound parameter to be set up is the optional filter section. Entering a "y" when prompted will access the filter modification section of this program.

The first selection is filter mode. Since the three modes may be mixed, valid inputs are between 16 and 112. Note that this input also affects whether voice 3 will be in the audio path or not. Voice 3 will be in the audio path, unless de-selected. Entering a "0" will cause no change in this setting.

The next input controls the resonance of the filters you have chosen. Any value from 0 (lowest) to 15 (highest) is valid. After the filter has been set, you must choose which of the three voices will be sent through the filter. Entering a "0" will cause all voices to *bypass* the filter. Entering a "7" (maximum) will process all three voices through.

The last filter setting is the optional modulation setting. This input will determine whether voice 3, or its ADSR generator will cause a variation in the filter cut-off frequency. Using this modulation will cause the filter's Fc to be continuously changed during the playing of a note. Entering a "0" will choose no modulation; a 1 or 2 will choose a modulation, as described by the program.

The A/D, S/R, and Pulse Width settings are, as explained in the *User's Guide*, numbers from 0 to 255. Values *above* 255 will cause the Program to stop with an ILLEGAL QUANTITY error.

The Tempo input value can be any positive value from .1 to anything. 50 seems to be the slowest bearable speed.

The waveforms are selected as shown in the *User's Guide*. Note the addition of Ring Modulation and Sync capabilities. Ring modulation is used to produce bell-like tones, gongs and other clangorous sounds.

After entering the waveforms, the set up of the SID synthesizer is complete. The next section of the program is used to enter the music notes for playing.

Each note is defined by entering two characters. The first character defines the note's letter value (A–G). The second character is a number, from 0 to 7, which defines the note's octave. Accidental notes (sharps and flats) are also available. To enter sharps simply use the shifted letter of the note; i.e., F-sharp, in the fifth octave, would be entered as F5. The natural F, in the same octave would be entered as f5. To enter flats, you must first convert the note to its equivalent sharp: G-flat in the fourth octave becomes F-sharp in the fourth octave, or F4. To convert flats to their equivalent sharps, use the MUSIC NOTE VALUES chart. Appendix M, pages 152–154 in the *User's Guide*. First, find the natural of the flatted note. Next, find the note directly above the natural. This is the note you want. Note that C and F do not have flats and B and E do not have sharps.

All three voice note values are entered in sequence, along with the optional Fc, on one line. The Fc input can be skipped by using the RETURN key. Do this *only* if you have selected a filter modulation source, or are not using the filter at all. Even if only one voice is using the filter, you must enter an Fc value (0–255) for each line. The only other option is to enter a − 1. This will instruct the computer to enter a random number into the Fc memory for that line.

You have a maximum of 500 such lines to program music data into. If your song takes up less than 500 lines, entering "st" (lower case as shown) will instruct the computer to stop accepting music line inputs. The computer will then begin to compile the music lines. This can take quite a long time, if your song is very long. Once the music has been compiled, the computer will instruct you to hit RETURN to begin the music playing routine.

As the music begins, a control code menu will be displayed. The music will play over and over again, unless you hit the "W" key. Note that all these codes are entered without using the RETURN key; the GET instruction is used to input a keystroke. Also note that the computer will finish playing the music before responding to the command.

The "M" command (Modify set-up) will allow you to re-program the SID chip's registers, while retaining the music data or song. If you only want to change *one* of the settings, hitting RETURN instead of entering data will cause the previous setting to remain unaltered. After modifying the synthesizer, you'll need to hit RETURN to re-play the song.

The "Q" command is used only when you wish to end the program. The "Q" key will allow you to use the RUN/STOP key to terminate, without having to listen to the last note played drone endlessly on.

The "E" key is used to enter the Edit mode. The "Note #" input directs the computer to the correct note line. To review two or more lines in sequence, enter "n" in response to the "CORRECT NOTE?" prompt. The computer will then ask for another note line.

To edit a certain line, type "y" for the prompt, then re-type the line, making the proper corrections. To exit the edit mode, type in "e" instead of "y" or "n". This will cause the music output section to begin again.

PROGRAM HIGHLIGHTS

Line 1 puts the computer in the upper/lower case display mode. Lines 5 and 6 set up the 10 variables used to store up to 500 lines of music input. Three string variables (v1$, v2$ and v3$) hold the note values for the three voices. Six variables are needed to hold the high- and low-frequency numbers for each of the three voices. FH(x) is used to store the Fc of the filter, when necessary.

Lines 7–9 are used to set up the functions which convert the alphanumeric note values (note letter/octave number) to the corresponding high and low frequency values for the SID chip. In line 10, variable A is used to hold the starting address of the SID. Line 11 calls the subroutine starting at line 580. This is the filter set-up section. At line 670, the program returns to line 15, the rest of the synthesizer set-up routine. The numbers are POKEd to their proper SID register to program the sound.

Line 36 insures that the music input section will be bypassed in the event that the user is only modifying the initial set-up. Line 37 clears the screen to prepare for the music input section. The music input loop is from lines 40 to 70. Line 50 detects when the user wishes to stop entering data. Lines 80 to 140 are the music compiling lines. The method used to determine the proper high and low frequency values is a software simulation of top octave generation. Data lines 918–945 contain the high/low frquency values of the highest 12 notes available. Lower octave numbers are mathematically derived from these values by dividing by 2 for every octave lowered.

Line 141 is the beginning of the playback section. The menu is displayed (lines 142–146). Lines 150–220 do the necessary work in order to play the music. Lines 225 to 320 determine which menu selection was chosen and perform the appropriate actions.

PROGRAM LISTING

```
printchr$(14)
dimv1$(500),v2$(500),v3$(500),h1(500),h2(500),h3(500),l1(500)
diml2(500),l3(500),fh(500)
deffnz1(y0)=int(y0*(1/(2↑(7-val(right$(v1$(fd),1))))))
deffnz2(y1)=int(y1*(1/(2↑(7-val(right$(v2$(fd),1))))))
deffnz3(y2)=int(y2*(1/(2↑(7-val(right$(v3$(fd),1))))))
0 a=54272:pokea+24,15:pokea+21,0:pokea+23,0
1 gosub580
5 input"A/D1,S/R1";o1,o2
6 input"A/D2,S/R2";o3,o4
7 input"A/D3,S/R3";o5,o6
8 input"Voice 1 pulse width Hi, Lo";p1,p2
9 input"Voice 2 pulse width Hi, Lo";p3,p4
0 input"Voice 3 pulse width Hi, Lo";p5,p6
1 print"Tempo";:inputdn
4 pokea+5,o1:pokea+6,o2
5 pokea+12,o3:pokea+13,o4
0 pokea+19,o5:pokea+20,o6
1 pokea+3,p2:pokea+2,p1:pokea+10,p4:pokea+9,p3
2 pokea+17,p6:pokea+16,p5
5 input"W1,W2,W3";t1,t2,t3:t4=t1-1:t5=t2-1:t6=t3-1
6 ifcc$="m"then141
7 print""
```

```
40 forn=1to500
45 print"Note ";n;tab(9);
50 input"V1";v1$(n):ifv1$(n)="st"thenln=n:n=500:v1$(n)="":
      goto70
54 printtab(17);:input"V2";v2$(n)
55 printtab(25);"V3";:inputv3$(n)
56 printtab(32);"Fc";:inputfh(n)
60 iffh(n)=-1thenfh(n)=int(rnd(0)*255)+1
70 next
80 forfd=1toln
85 fordc=1to13
90 read nc$,h,l
95 ifnc$="end"then90sub1000
100 ifnc$=left$(v1$(fd),1)thenh1(fd)=fnz1(h):11(fd)=fnz1(l)
110 ifnc$=left$(v2$(fd),1)thenh2(fd)=fnz2(h):12(fd)=fnz2(l)
120 ifnc$=left$(v3$(fd),1)thenh3(fd)=fnz3(h):13(fd)=fnz3(l)
130 next
140 next
141 print"Hit RETURN to play";:inputen$
142 printtab(5)"w -- Wait mode"
143 printtab(5)"q -- Quit (before break)"
144 printtab(5)"e -- Edit Music"
145 printtab(5)"m -- Modify set up"
146 printtab(5)"r -- RePlay Music after q or w"
149 pokea+4,0:pokea+11,0:pokea+18,0
150 forx=0toln-1
155 pokea+4,t1:pokea+11,t2:pokea+18,t3
160 pokea+1,h1(x):pokea,11(x):ifh1(x)+11(x)=0thenpokea+4,t4
170 pokea+8,h2(x):pokea+7,12(x):ifh2(x)+12(x)=0thenpokea+11,t5
180 pokea+15,h3(x):pokea+14,13(x):
        ifh3(x)+13(x)=0thenpokea+18,t6
190 if(m1<>1)or(m1<>2)thenpokea+22,fh(x)
200 formm=1todn*10
201 ifm1=1thenpokea+22,peek(a+27)
202 ifm1=2thenpokea+22,peek(a+28)
210 nextmm
220 nextx
225 getcc$
230 ifcc$="w"thenpokea+4,0:pokea+11,0:pokea+18,0:goto300
231 ifcc$="q"then330
235 ifcc$="e"thenpokea+4,0:pokea+11,0:pokea+18,0:goto400
236 ifcc$="m"thenpokea+4,0:pokea+11,0:pokea+18,0:goto11
240 goto150
300 getc2$:ifc2$=""then300
310 ifc2$="r"then240
320 goto300
330 pokea+4,0:pokea+11,0:pokea+18,0:goto300
400 print"Music Edit Mode"
410 input"Which note # ";nn
420 print"Note ";nn;tab(9);
430 print"V1";v1$(nn)
440 printtab(17);"V2";v2$(nn)
450 printtab(25);"V3";v3$(nn)
460 printtab(32);"Fc";fh(nn)
```

```
470 input"Correct note (y) or (n) or [e]scape";yn$
480 ifyn$="n"then400
485 ifyn$="e"then141
490 ifyn$="y"then500
495 print"**Incorrect response":goto470
500 print"⬛Enter new information:"
510 print"Note ";nn;tab(9);
520 input"V1";v1$(nn):ifv1$(nn)="st"thenln=nn:n=500:
     v1$(nn)="":goto561
530 printtab(17);:input"▨V2";v2$(nn)
540 printtab(25);"▨V3";:inputv3$(nn)
550 printtab(32);"▨Fc";:inputfh(nn)
555 fd=nn
560 iffh(nn)=-1thenfh(nn)=int(rnd(0)*255)+1
561 fordc=1to13
562 read nc$,h,l
563 ifnc$="end"thengosub1000
564 ifnc$=left$(v1$(fd),1)thenh1(fd)=fnz1(h):l1(fd)=fnz1(l)
565 ifnc$=left$(v2$(fd),1)thenh2(fd)=fnz2(h):l2(fd)=fnz2(l)
566 ifnc$=left$(v3$(fd),1)thenh3(fd)=fnz3(h):l3(fd)=fnz3(l)
567 next
570 goto141
580 print"⬛⬛⬛Do you want to alter the filter"
581 input"⬛settings (y) or (n)";gz$:ifgz$="n"thenreturn
585 print"⬛⬛▶▶—Filter Set up—":print
590 print"Voice 3 off (128)lhi pass (64)":print
591 print"   band pass (32)llo pass (16)"
592 print"Add the numbers in () and enter":
     input"  your choice";fs
593 fs=fs+15:pokea+24,fs
595 input"Enter resonance value (0-15)";rz:rz=rz*16
600 print"Filter ← Voice 3 (4)"
601 print"Filter ← Voice 2 (2)"
602 print"Filter ← Voice 1 (1)"
605 print"Add the numbers in () and enter";:inputfz:rz=rz+fz
610 pokea+23,rz
620 print"Modulation from Voice 3:":
     print"Oscillator (1) or A/D S/R (2)";
625 inputm1
670 return
899 stop
900 rem ***top octave generation****
910 data a,230,176,"G",217,189,g,205,133
920 data "F",193,252,f,183,25,e,172,210
930 data "D",163,31,d,153,247,"C",145,83
940 data c,137,43,b,129,120,"A",122,52
945 data end,0,0
950 rem "A"=a#:"C"=c#:"D"=d#:"F"=f#:"G"=g#
1000 restore
1005 return
```

15. Pirate

You are a modern-day pirate. For the past ten years, you've been collecting various treasures and storing them in your hideouts. Your time is almost up, though; the Coast Police have found you out. A massive search has begun to find and recover the stolen goods. The Police also wish to put an end to your career.

Altogether, you've stashed away over $25,000. You must recover at least $15,000 in treasure before you leave for ports unknown.

PLAYING

This game, like SWORDSMASTER, can be controlled from either the keyboard, or with joystick control. Listing 2 shows the necessary changes for joystick control.

For keyboard controls, the "." key moves your ship to the right, while the "," key moves it to the left. To move up, use the "+" key; "-" moves you down screen.

The object of the game is to uncover $1,500 worth of treasure from each screen, or cove, area. Your treasure is represented by the red diamonds; your ship by the circle, and the police ship is shown by the "X". You can *not* pick up treasure which has been confiscated by the police; this is shown when the diamond is changed into a square.

PROGRAM HIGHLIGHTS

Line 4 seeds the random number generator and resets the treasure counter, TR. The subroutine beginning at line 1000 plays the game's theme song, the Sailor's Hornpipe. The screen selection subroutine, starting at line 2000, determines which screen (cove) area will be displayed. The screen chosen depends on the level of play the player achieves. Line 2010 may be altered as desired to change the order in which the screens are chosen. Valid line numbers are: 499, 2199, 2299, 2399, and 2499. Any sequence of these line numbers is acceptable, as long as the sequence contains the line numbers (one for each level of play).

Line 20 initializes four screen memory pointers which are updated, according to both the player's and the computer's moves. PX is the variable which keeps track of the player's current position; CX holds the computer's current position. After every move, these values are transferred to their companion variables, OP and OC. These variables hold the old positions.

Line 30 puts the right screen display code into the pre-assigned screen memory location to start off the game. Line 40 generates a random number, then checks land flag F8. If F8 is set (equal to 1), the last attempted move is considered to be invalid. In that case, the random number is used to choose a new route. If no land was sighted on the prior move, lines 41–46 come in to play. These lines constitute a low intelligence radar simulator. The first half of these lines subtract the player's known position from the computer's location. The second half of these lines convert the data obtained into a movement which will cause an approach to the player's pirate ship. For more details, see figure 1. From these lines, the computer can detect the best possible move, out of eight, in which to go in order to catch the player. The player's input routine is from line 70 to line 85.

The subroutine in lines 300–350 checks to see if the land mass detected by the computer has pirate treasure hidden. If there is, the treasure is confiscated, or graphically closed off to the pirate. Lines 400–440 detect treasure for the pirate. If treasure is found, it is transferred to the pirate vessel.

Figure 1.

Example: Suppose the Coast Police are at location 1324, the Pirate at location 1402. Therefore:

$$MF = (1324 - 1402)/40 = -1.95$$
and $$MF = (1324 - 1402)/39 = -2$$
and $$MF = (1324 - 1402)/41 = -1.902$$

Then the only integer result is -2, in the middle above. This indicates that either line 43 or 44 in the listing will be correct. Since the sign is negative $(SGN(-2) = -1)$, line 44 is true. Therefore, the Pirate is somewhere down and to the left of the Coast Police ship.

PROGRAM LISTING

```
4 W=RND(-TI):W=0:TR=0
5 LV=10:GOSUB1000:N1=1
10 PRINT"⊐":GOSUB2000
15 POKE53281,15
20 PX=1921:CX=1913:OC=1913:OP=1921:MM=0
30 POKEPX,81:POKECX,86
40 MC=INT(RND(0)*8)+1:IFF8=1THENF8=0:GOTO50
41 MF=(CX-PX)/40:IFMF=INT(MF)THENIFSGN(MF)=-1THENMC=2
42 MF=(CX-PX)/40:IFMF=INT(MF)THENIFSGN(MF)=1THENMC=1
43 MF=(CX-PX)/39:IFMF=INT(MF)THENIFSGN(MF)=1THENMC=7
44 MF=(CX-PX)/39:IFMF=INT(MF)THENIFSGN(MF)=-1THENMC=8
45 MF=(CX-PX)/41:IFMF=INT(MF)THENIFSGN(MF)=-1THENMC=3
46 MF=(CX-PX)/41:IFMF=INT(MF)THENIFSGN(MF)=1THENMC=4
```

```
50 IFMC=1THENCX=CX+40
51 IFMC=2THENCX=CX-40
52 IFMC=3THENCX=CX+41
53 IFMC=4THENCX=CX-41
54 IFMC=5THENCX=CX+1
55 IFMC=6THENCX=CX-1
56 IFMC=7THENCX=CX-39
57 IFMC=8THENCX=CX+39
58 IFPEEK(CX)<>32THENCX=OC:POKECX,86:F8=1:GOTO40
59 IFCX<1185THENCX=OC:GOTO40
60 IFCX>1983THENCX=OC:GOTO40
61 GOSUB300
65 POKECX,86:POKECX+54272,7:POKEOC,32:OC=CX
66 IF(CX<5+PX)AND(CX>PX-5)THENGOSUB700
67 IF(CX=40+PX)OR(CX=PX-40)THENGOSUB750
70 GETA$:GOSUB400:IFA$=""THEN72
71 PF$=A$
72 IFPF$=","THENPX=PX+1
73 IFPF$=","THENPX=PX-1
74 IFPF$="+"THENPX=PX-40
75 IFPF$="-"THENPX=PX+40
76 POKE54276,32
77 IFPEEK(PX)<>32THENPX=OP:POKEPX,81:GOTO50
78 IFPX<1185THENPX=OP:GOTO70
79 IFPX>1983THENPX=OP:GOTO70
80 POKEPX,81:POKEPX+54272,1:POKEOP,32:OP=PX
85 GOTO40
300 IFPEEK(CX+40)=90THENPOKECX+40,160:MM=MM+1
310 IFPEEK(CX-40)=90THENPOKECX-40,160:MM=MM+1
320 IFPEEK(CX-1)=90THENPOKECX-1,160:MM=MM+1
330 IFPEEK(CX+1)=90THENPOKECX+1,160:MM=MM+1
335 PRINT"        HIDE OUTS LEFT:        ";17-MM
340 IFMM>16THENMM=0:GOTO900
350 RETURN
400 IFPEEK(PX+40)=90THENTR=TR+50:POKEPX+40,78:MM=MM+1:GOSUB45
410 IFPEEK(PX-40)=90THENTR=TR+50:POKEPX-40,77:MM=MM+1:GOSUB45
420 IFPEEK(PX-1)=90THENTR=TR+50:POKEPX-1,78:MM=MM+1:GOSUB450
430 IFPEEK(PX+1)=90THENTR=TR+50:POKEPX+1,77:MM=MM+1:GOSUB450
435 PRINT"        TREASURE: $        ";TR:
        IFTR=(500*N1)THEN900
436 PRINT"        HIDE OUTS LEFT:        ";17-MM
437 IFMM>16THENMM=0:GOTO900
440 RETURN
450 T9=TR/10:IFT9>255THENT9=10
451 POKE54296,15:POKE54277,96:POKE54278,250:POKE54273,3:
        POKE54272,T9
455 POKE54276,33:RETURN
498 REM TOP CORNER=1189
499 PRINT"     "
500 PRINT"                                               "
501 PRINT"                                               "
502 PRINT"                                               "
503 PRINT"                                               "
504 PRINT"                                               "
505 PRINT"                                               "
506 PRINT"                                               "
507 PRINT"                                               "
```

```
08 PRINT" ▓▓▓▓▓▓▓▓+▫          ▓▭▭▭▭▫          ▓▨▨ ▓▓▓▓▓▓▓"
09 PRINT" ▓▓▓▓▓▓▨ ▓▫          ▨+▓▓+▓          ▨+▓▓▓▓▓▓▓"
10 PRINT" ▓▓▓▓▓▓▨ ▓▫          ▨+▓▓▫           ▨+▓▓▓▓▓▓▓"
11 PRINT" ▓▓▓▓▓▓▓+▫           ▓▼▫             ▓▓▓▓▓▓▓▓"
12 PRINT" ▓▓▓▓▓▓▓▫                          ▓▓▓▓▓▓▓▓▓"
13 PRINT" ▓▓▓▓▓▓▓ ▫                       ▓▓ ▓▓▓▓▓▓▓▓"
14 PRINT" ▓▓▓▓▓▓▓+▫                        ▓▓▓▓▓▓▓▓▓"
15 PRINT" ▓▓▓▓▓▓▓▫   ▓▭▭▨+▓▭▭▫         ▓▭▭▭▨▼▓▓▓▓▓▓▓▓"
16 PRINT" ▓▓▓▓▓▓▓+▫   ▓▓▓▓▓▓▓ ▫          ▓▓▓▓▓▓▓▓▓▓▓▓"
17 PRINT" ▓▓▓▓▓▓▓▫    ▓▓ ▓▓▓▓▫         ▨+▓▓▓▓▓▓▓▓▓▓▓"
18 PRINT" ▓▓▓▓▓▓▓+▫    ▨+▓▓▓▓ ▫     ▓▭▭▭▭_▓▓▓▓▓▓▓▓▓▓"
19 PRINT" ▓▓▓▓▓▓▓▓▓▓▓▓▓▓▓▓▓▓▓▓▓▓▓▓▓▓▓▓▓▓▓▓▓▓▓▓▓▓▓▓▓▓▓▓▓▓▓▓▓▓▓▓▓◼"
20 RETURN
30 IFPX>CXTHENMO=1
31 IFPX<CXTHENMO=-1
35 FORCI=CXTOPXSTEPMO:POKECI,86:POKECI+(MO*-1),32:NEXT
36 POKEPX,87:GOTO5000
50 IFPX<CXTHENMO=40
51 IFPX>CXTHENMO=-40
57 FORCI=CXTOPXSTEPMO:POKECI,86:POKECI+(MO*-1),32:NEXT
58 POKEPX,87:GOTO5000
90 IFTR>5000THEN5000
00 IFN1=10THEN5000
20 PRINT"⬛":N1=N1+1:PRINT"▨▨▨▨▨▨▨▨▨▨LEVEL▨";N1
30 FORGG=1TO2500:NEXT:RESTORE:GOTO10
000 REM ********THEME SONG********
001 REM ***(SAILOR'S HORNPIPE)***
002 REM ******AS PLAYED BY*******
003 REM **THE ANCIENT MARINERS***
004 REM **FIFE AND DRUM CORPS****
010 POKE54296,15:POKE54277,67:POKE54278,64
020 READL,H,L2
025 IFL=-1THENPOKE54276,0:RESTORE:RETURN
030 POKE54276,33
040 POKE54273,H:POKE54272,L2
050 FORTY=1TOL:NEXT:POKE54276,32
060 GOTO1020
00 DATA 62,51,97,62,48,127,124,51,97,124,25,177,124,25,177
10 DATA62,38,126,62,34,75,62,32,94,62,38,126,124,51,97
20 DATA62,51,97,62,64,188,62,57,172,62,51,97,124,57,172
30 DATA124,28,214,62,28,214,62,32,94,62,28,214,62,25,177
40 DATA62,24,63,62,28,214,124,38,126,124,38,126,62,43,52
50 DATA62,48,127,62,51,97,62,48,127,62,43,52,62,38,126
60 DATA62,43,52,62,38,126,62,34,75,62,32,94,62,34,75
70 DATA 62,32,94,62,28,214,62,25,177,62,28,214,62,25,177
80 DATA 62,24,63,62,21,154,62,19,63,62,25,177,62,24,63
90 DATA 62,28,214,62,25,177,62,32,94,62,28,214,62,34,75
00 DATA 250,32,94,255,25,177,500,25,177,-1,-1,-1
00 SC=SC+1:REM SCREEN SELECTION COMMITTEE
10 ON SC GOSUB 499,499,2199,2199,2299,2299,2399,2499,
      2399,2499
15 IFSC=11THENGOTO5000
20 RETURN
99 PRINT"⬛▨▨▨"
00 PRINT" ▓▓▓▓▓▓▓▓▓▓▓▓▓▓▓▓▓▓▓▓▓▓▓▓▓▓▓▓▓▓▓▓▓▓▓▓▓▓▓▓▓▓▓▓▓▓▓▓▓"
01 PRINT"▓▓▓▓▓▓▼▬▬▬▬▬▬▬▓▓▓▓▓▓▨+▓▓   ▓▓▓▓▓▓▓▓▓▓▓▓▓"
02 PRINT"▓▓▓▓▓▼▓▨+        +▓▼▓▓▓▓▓▓    ▓▓▓▓▓▓▓▓▓▓"
```

```
2203 PRINT"�" ...graphics...
2204 PRINT"▓ ...graphics...
2205 PRINT"▓ ...graphics...
2206 PRINT"▓ ...graphics...
2207 PRINT"▓ ...graphics...
2208 PRINT"▓ ...graphics...
2209 PRINT"▓ ...graphics...
2210 PRINT"▓ ...graphics...
2211 PRINT"▓ ...graphics...
2212 PRINT"▓ ...graphics...
2213 PRINT"▓ ...graphics...
2214 PRINT"▓ ...graphics...
2215 PRINT"▓ ...graphics...
2216 PRINT"▓ ...graphics...
2217 PRINT"▓ ...graphics...
2218 PRINT"▓ ...graphics...
2219 PRINT"▓ ...graphics...
2220 RETURN
2229 PRINT" ...graphics..."
2299 PRINT" ...graphics..."
2300 PRINT" ...graphics...
2301 PRINT" ...graphics...
2302 PRINT" ...graphics...
2303 PRINT" ...graphics...
2304 PRINT" ...graphics...
2305 PRINT" ...graphics...
2306 PRINT" ...graphics...
2307 PRINT" ...graphics...
2308 PRINT" ...graphics...
2309 PRINT" ...graphics...
2310 PRINT" ...graphics...
2311 PRINT" ...graphics...
2312 PRINT" ...graphics...
2313 PRINT" ...graphics...
2314 PRINT" ...graphics...
2315 PRINT" ...graphics...
2316 PRINT" ...graphics...
2317 PRINT" ...graphics...
2318 PRINT" ...graphics...
2319 PRINT" ...graphics...
2320 RETURN
2399 PRINT" ...graphics..."
2400 PRINT" ...graphics...
2401 PRINT" ...graphics...
2402 PRINT" ...graphics...
2403 PRINT" ...graphics...
2404 PRINT" ...graphics...
2405 PRINT" ...graphics...
2406 PRINT" ...graphics...
2407 PRINT" ...graphics...
2408 PRINT" ...graphics...
2409 PRINT" ...graphics...
2410 PRINT" ...graphics...
2411 PRINT" ...graphics...
2412 PRINT" ...graphics...
2413 PRINT" ...graphics...
```

```
2414 PRINT"                                                    "
2415 PRINT"                                                    "
2416 PRINT"                                                    "
2417 PRINT"                                                    "
2418 PRINT"                                                    "
2419 PRINT"                                                    "
2420 RETURN
2499 PRINT"            "
2500 PRINT"                                                    "
2501 PRINT"                                                    "
2502 PRINT"                                                    "
2503 PRINT"                                                    "
2504 PRINT"                                                    "
2505 PRINT"                                                    "
2506 PRINT"                                                    "
2507 PRINT"                                                    "
2508 PRINT"                                                    "
2509 PRINT"                                                    "
2510 PRINT"                                                    "
2511 PRINT"                                                    "
2512 PRINT"                                                    "
2513 PRINT"                                                    "
2514 PRINT"                                                    "
2515 PRINT"                                                    "
2516 PRINT"                                                    "
2517 PRINT"                                                    "
2518 PRINT"                                                    "
2519 PRINT"                                                    "
2520 RETURN
5000 PRINT"                            ":GOSUB1000
5010 PRINT"                                            "
5011 PRINT"                                            "
5012 PRINT"                                            "
5013 PRINT"                                            "
5014 PRINT"                                            "
5015 PRINT"                                            "
5016 PRINT:PRINT"                                            "
5017 PRINT:PRINT
5020 IFN1=10THENPRINT"     KING OF THE SEVEN SEAS "
5030 IFN1=9THENPRINT"     PRINCE OF PIRACY"
5040 IFN1=8THENPRINT"    KING OF SIX OF THE SEVEN SEAS"
5050 IFN1=7THENPRINT"    MASTER OF THE BRINY DEEP"
5060 IFN1=6THENPRINT"     A NOT VERY RICH PIRATE"
5070 IFN1=5THENPRINT"          FIRST   MATE"
5080 IFN1=4THENPRINT"          CABIN   BOY"
5090 IFN1<4THENPRINT"          LANDLUBBER"
5100 IFN1=1THENPRINT"        OR A COAST GUARD SPY!"
5110 PRINT"            "
```

LISTING 2 -- PIRATE JOYSTICK CONTROL

```
70 PZ=PEEK(56320):GOSUB400:IFPZ=127THEN72
71 PF=PZ
72 IFPF=119THENPX=PX+1
73 IFPF=123THENPX=PX-1
74 IFPF=126THENPX=PX-40
75 IFPF=125THENPX=PX+40
```

16. Take-Off

This program is a model plane flight simulator. You have control over the throttle speed, as well as the wing's flap angle. By adjusting these values in real-time, you are to successfully take off, make a short run, and land the plane. The Commodore 64's internal clock is used to time the flight. A different plane is used each time; a random number is used to set the plane's lift coefficient. This determines the speed and flap angle necessary to cause the plane to take off.

The controls for your "radio-controlled" plane are shown in figure 1.

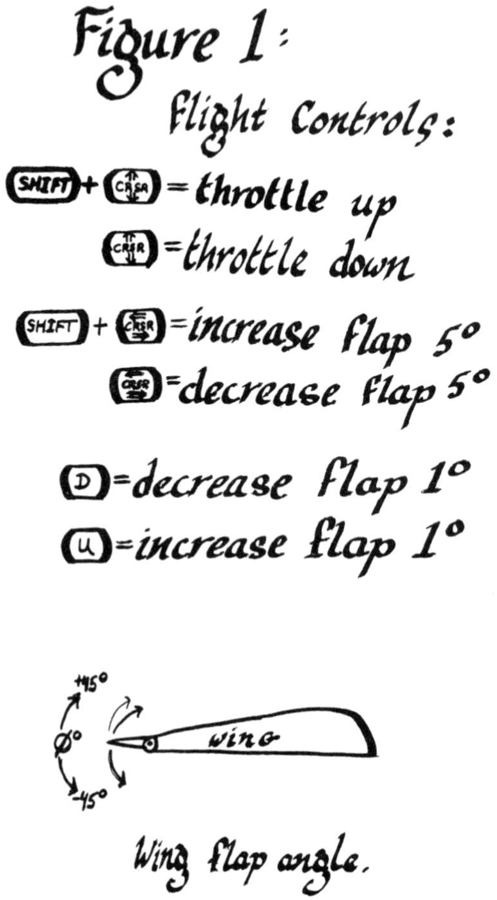

Figure 1 :

Flight Controls :

(SHIFT) + (CRSR ↑) = throttle up

(CRSR ↓) = throttle down

(SHIFT) + (CRSR →) = increase flap 5°

(CRSR ←) = decrease flap 5°

(D) = decrease flap 1°

(U) = increase flap 1°

Wing flap angle.

PROGRAM HIGHLIGHTS

Line 5 sets the background screen color to white. Line 7 sets the internal clock. Lines 10–49 take care of the sprites, determine the lift coefficient, and other sundry things.

The subroutine beginning at line 5000 POKEs in a small machine level program; used here more as a time saving device, than anything else. The machine level program is used to transfer the frequency numbers to the SID chip. It does so faster than BASIC can, and therefore speeds up the execution of the program.

The SYS9026 part of line 50 calls the machine program. Lines 50–91 input and decode the player's key depressions. The flap angle is determined in line 93. Line 98 displays both flap angle and speed. The sprite's Y position is determined by the formula in line 100. Lines 101–102 determine the pitch of the engine, based on the present speed of the plane, line 110 determines the x position. The background sprite is updated in lines 130–140, and line 150 jumps back to the beginning of the loop.

PROGRAM LISTING

```
5 POKE53281,1
6 PRINT"█████████████████████████████████████"                (37 spaces)
                                        "█"
7 TI$="000000":PRINT"███████TIME:  ";TI$
10 V=53248:POKEV+21,3:POKE2040,150:POKE2041,151
11 XP=20:YP=218:BX=240:POKEV+39,0:POKEV+40,14:
   CL=RND(0)*10:CL=INT(CL)/1000
12 IFCL<=0THEN11
13 PRINT"██INITIAL LIFT COEFFICIENT:";CL
14 OP=YP
15 POKEV+29,3:POKEV+23,2:POKEV+27,2
20 FORP=0TO62STEP3:POKE9664+P,0:POKE9665+P,255:
   POKE9666+P,0:NEXT
30 FORP=0TO62:READQ:POKE9600+P,Q:NEXT
40 POKEV,XP:POKEV+1,YP:POKEV+2,BX:POKEV+3,200
45 GOSUB5000
50 SYS9026:GETA$
55 PRINT"███████TIME:  ";TI$
60 IFA$="]"THENSP=SP+3
70 IFA$="█"THENSP=SP-3
75 IFSP<0THENSP=0
80 IFA$="U"THENCL=CL+.001:IFNC=1THENCL=CL-.001
81 IFA$="█"THENCL=CL+.005:IFNC=1THENCL=CL-.005
90 IFA$="D"THENCL=CL-.001:IFNC=1THENCL=CL+.001
91 IFA$="█"THENCL=CL-.005:IFNC=1THENCL=CL+.005
93 FA=INT(CL*1000)-(10*CL):FA=INT(FA)
```

```
94 IFFA<-45THENFA=-45:NC=1
95 IFFA>45THENFA=45:NC=1
96 IFSP>399THENSP=399
97 PRINT"█████████                                    "
98 PRINT"█████████SPEED:";SP;"   F.A.:";FA;" DEGREES"
99 IF(FA>-45)OR(FA<45)THENNC=0
100 YP=YP-((CL*1.68*(SP↑2))/100)+10
101 SF=(SP↑1.09)+600:HF=INT(SF/256):LF=SF-(256*HF)
102 POKE9025,HF:POKE9024,LF:SYS9026
104 IF(YP>205)AND(SP>160)THENGOSUB6000
105 IFYP<50THENYP=50
106 IFYP>218THENYP=218
107 IF(YP<90)AND(SP>100)THEN6100
110 XP=XP+(.0032*SP):IFXP>240THENXP=240
115 IFXP>125THENPRINT"████████            LAND THE PLANE."
116 IF(XP>125)AND(YP<150)THENPRINT
    "█████████**DANGER** LAND THE PLANE."
117 IF(XP>190)AND(YP>205)AND(SP<161)THENGOTO700
120 POKEV,XP:POKEV+1,YP
130 BX=BX-(SP/1.894):IFBX<10THENBX=240
140 POKEV+2,BX
150 GOTO50
700 PRINT"██████████SUCCESSFUL LANDING."
710 POKE54296,0:END
900 DATA 0,0,0,0,0,0,0,0,0,0,0,0,0,0,0,0,0,0,0
910 DATA 0,0,224,0,3,192,0,15,130,0,124,130
920 DATA 0,8,254,0,8,254,0,11,254,64
930 DATA 31,218,240,127,194,249,255,130
940 DATA 255,255,192,255,195,64,254,1,192
950 DATA 112,1,192,0,1,192
5000 FORML=9026TO9048
5010 READPD:POKEML,PD
5011 NEXT
5020 SI=54272
5030 POKESI+24,15:POKESI+5,80:POKESI+6,240
5040 POKESI+1,18:POKESI,1:POKESI+4,33
5060 RETURN
5100 DATA 169,0,141,4,212,173,65,35,141,1,212,173
5110 DATA 64,35,141,0,212,169,33,141,4,212,96
6000 PRINT"████ AIRSPEED WAS TOO FAST FOR PROPER"
6010 PRINT" TAKE-OFF/LANDING. PLANE DAMAGED."
6020 GOTO6120
6100 PRINT"████ SPEEDY ASCENT CAUSES YOU TO LOOP:"
6110 PRINT" YOU HAVE LOST CONTROL OF YOUR PLANE."
6120 POKE53269,0:POKE54296,0
6130 FORTT=1TO3600:NEXT:RUN
```

17. Wildlife Warden

You have been hired as the overall Manager of a wildlife sanctuary. The area (about 50 square miles) has been landscaped and is now ready to be populated. The area has been designed to accommodate the following species: bear, deer, raccoon, red fox, and rabbit. Additionally, toads will be needed as food for certain of the predators (they will also help to cut down the population of insects).

The food chain that will occur is shown in figure 1. The problem you must solve is; how many animals of each species are needed to provide an ecologically balanced system?

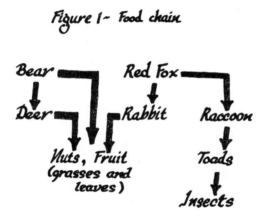

Figure 1- Food chain

PLAYING

The first step is to enter the initial numbers of each species. Then follow the prompt to cycle through each section. At the start of each new year, you have the option of opening a hunting season. You must enter either "C" (closed to hunters) or "O" (open season). If you elect to open hunting, you must then enter the number of hunters allowed in the park.

PROGRAM HIGHLIGHTS

Line 10 defines two functions which are to be used repeatedly in the program; function D is used in the overpopulated calculation; function R provides the basis for deriving random numbers. Line 20 resets the month/year counter and closes the hunting season. Line 25 sets up the initial number of insects, fruit, and nuts available for consumption by the animals.

Lines 30 to 90 input the initial number of each animal. Line 110 contains the month/year counter. This line also calls the subroutine to open or close the hunting season. Lines 120 to 180 are used to call various subroutines. The subroutines at 940 and 1000 are called once on each line. The remaining subroutines (at 300, 390, 490, 570, 700, and 830) are identified by their subsequent text messages.

The subroutine beginning on line 940 stores the animal totals in temporary variables T1 through T9. After this subroutine, the animal numbers will be altered by each statistic modifier (births, deaths, etc.) The variables T1–T9 are necessary to determine the numbers of each species lost due to the statistic subroutines.

The subroutine at line 1000 calls two other routines. The animal numbers are prevented from becoming negative by the first subroutine (1140). The second, at 970, compares the "before" data (in T1 through T9) with the animal numbers left after statistical modification. The difference between the two is displayed when this subroutine returns to line 1005.

After each of the statistical modification subroutines has been executed, the monthly totals are PRINTed. The initial monthly totals (held in B1–B9) are displayed, along with the end of month totals. After this, the cycle starts anew.

PROGRAM LISTING

```
5 POKE53281,1
10 DEF FND(DV)=DV/100:DEF FNR(R0)=INT(RND(0)*R0)+1
20 MO=0:YR=0:H$="C"
25 I=41000:F=21000:N=40000
30 PRINT"◤▩▮▮▮▮▮INPUT INITIAL NUMBERS"
40 INPUT"   NUMBER OF BEARS ";BR
50 INPUT"   NUMBER OF DEER ";DR
60 INPUT"   NUMBER OF RACCOON ";RC
70 INPUT"   NUMBER OF RED FOX ";RF
80 INPUT"   NUMBER OF RABBITS ";RB
90 INPUT"   NUMBER OF TOADS ";TD
110 MO=MO+1:IFMO=13THENMO=1:YR=YR+1:GOSUB1100
111 PRINT"◤▩▩";TAB(5);"MONTH: ";MO;" YEAR: ";YR
114 GOSUB1140
115 GOSUB995
120 GOSUB940:GOSUB300:PRINT"◤▩▩▩▩";TAB(12);"BIRTHS:":GOSUB1000
130 IFH$="O"THENGOSUB940:GOSUB830:PRINT"◤▩▩▩▩";TAB(12);
          "HUNTERS KILL:":GOSUB1000
140 IFH$="C"THENPRINT"HUNTING SEASON CLOSED"
150 GOSUB940:GOSUB390:PRINT"◤▩▩▩▩";TAB(9);"NATURAL DEATHS:":GOSUB100
160 GOSUB940:GOSUB700:PRINT"◤▩▩▩▩";TAB(9);"STARVATION:    ":GOSUB100
170 GOSUB940:GOSUB570:PRINT"◤▩▩▩▩";TAB(9);"OVERPOPULATION:":GOSUB100
180 GOSUB940:GOSUB490:PRINT"◤▩▩▩▩";TAB(9);"DEATH BY PREDATOR:":
          GOSUB1000
```

```
185 GOSUB1140
190 PRINT"JOMMONTH'S TOTALS"
200 PRINT"     ANIMAL    STARTED     ENDED"
205 PRINT"      TYPE      WITH        WITH"
210 PRINT"    :JBEARS:    ";B1;TAB(25);INT(BR)
215 PRINT"     ZDEER:     ";B2;TAB(25);INT(DR)
220 PRINT"   ZRACCOON:    ";B3;TAB(25);INT(RC)
230 PRINT"   ZRED FOX:    ";B4;TAB(25);INT(RF)
240 PRINT"    :RABBIT:    ";B5;TAB(25);INT(RB)
250 PRINT"    ZTOADS:     ";B6;TAB(25);INT(TD)
260 PRINT"   ZINSECTS:    ";B7;TAB(25);INT(I)
270 PRINT"     FRUIT:     ";B8;TAB(25);INT(F)
280 PRINT"     NUTS:      ";B9;TAB(25);INT(N)
285 PRINT"XOMMHIT ANY KEY TO CONTINUE"
290 GETZZ$:IFZZ$=""THEN290
295 GOTO110
300 REM BIRTH FIGURES
310 IFMO=6THENIFBR>1THENBR=BR+((BR/2)*FNR(2))
320 IFMO=4THENIFDR>1THENDR=DR+((DR/2)*FNR(2))
330 IF(MO=6)OR(MO=3)THENIFRC>1THENRC=RC+((RC/2)*FNR(5))
340 IF(MO=3)OR(MO=10)THENIFRF>1THENRF=RF+((RF/2)*FNR(4))
350 IF((MO>1)AND(MO<11))AND(MO/2=INT(MO/2))THENIFRB>1
        THENRB=RB+((RB/2)*FNR(8))
360 IF(MO=3)OR(MO=6)OR(MO=9)OR(MO=11)THENIFTD>1
        THENTD=TD+((TD/2)*FNR(3))
370 IF(MO>2)AND(MO<11)THENI=I+FNR(6000):N=N+FNR(4300)
380 IF(MO>2)AND(MO<10)THENF=F+FNR(5500)
385 RETURN
390 REM NATURAL DEATH RATES
400 IFYR>7THENBR=BR-FNR(3)
410 IFYR>6THENDR=DR-FNR(2)
420 IFYR>5THENRC=RC-FNR(6)
430 IFYR>4THENRF=RF-FNR(4):RB=RB-FNR(15)
440 IFYR>2THENTD=TD-FNR(5)
450 IF(MO=6)OR(MO=12)THENI=I-FNR(1000)+500
460 IF(MO>9)THENN=N-FNR(3500)
470 IF(MO>9)THENF=F-FNR(4500)
480 RETURN
490 REM NATURAL PREDATOR -- PREY COSTS
500 IFDR>0THENDR=DR-(.0416*BR)
510 IFN>0THENN=N-(25*BR)
515 IFF>0THENF=F-(26*BR)
520 IFN>0THENN=N-(27*DR)
525 IFF>0THENF=F-(16*DR)
530 IFTD>0THENTD=TD-(2*RC)
535 IFI>0THENI=I-(26*RC)
540 IFRC>0THENRC=RC-(6*RF)
545 IFRB>0THENRB=RB-(5*RF)
550 IFN>0THENN=N-(11*RB)
555 IFF>0THENF=F-(11*RB)
560 IFI>0THENI=I-(12*TD)
565 RETURN
570 REM OVERPOPULATION EFFECTS
590 OB=BR-120:OD=DR-150:OC=RC-500:OF=RF-300:OX=RB-600:OT=TD-1200
600 IFOB>0THENBR=BR-(FND(OB)*70)
610 IFOD>0THENDR=DR-(FND(OD)*90)
620 IFOC>0THENRC=RC-(FND(OC)*130)
630 IFOF>0THENRF=RF-(FND(OF)*100)
640 IFOX>0THENRB=RB-(FND(OX)*110)
650 IFOT>0THENTD=TD-(FND(OT)*170)
660 OI=I-15000:IFOI>0THENI=I-(FND(OI)*120)
670 OF=F-10000:IFOF>0THENF=F-(FND(OF)*120)
```

```
680 OY=N-30000:IFOY>0THENN=N-(FND(OY)*120)
690 RETURN
700 REM STARVATION FACTORS
710 IFDR<(.0416*BR)THENBR=BR-(.1*BR)
720 IFN<(600*BR)THENBR=BR-(.1*BR)
730 IFF<(300*BR)THENBR=BR-(.1*BR)
740 IFN<(700*DR)THENDR=DR-(.1*DR)
750 IFF<(200*DR)THENDR=DR-(.1*DR)
760 IFTD<(200*RC)THENRC=RC-(.1*RC)
770 IFI<(400*RC)THENRC=RC-(.1*RC)
780 IFRC<(10*RF)THENRF=RF-(.1*RF)
790 IFRB<(90*RF)THENRF=RF-(.1*RF)
800 IFN<(500*RB)THENRB=RB-(.2*RB)
810 IFF<(50*RB)THENRB=RB-(.1*RB)
820 RETURN
830 REM HUNTING SEASON IS OPEN
835 IF(MO<2)OR(MO>7)THENRETURN
840 IFBR>0THENBR=BR-(H*FNR(2))
850 IFDR>0THENDR=DR-(H*FNR(2))
860 IFRC>0THENRC=RC-(H*FNR(4))
870 IFRF>0THENRF=RF-(H*FNR(4))
880 IFRB>0THENRB=RB-(H*FNR(5))
890 IFTD>100THENTD=TD-(H*FNR(2)):REM HUNTERS STEP ON TOADS
900 IFI>10000THENI=I-(H*FNR(30)):REM HUNTERS USE INSECT REPELLENT
910 IFN>9000THENN=N-(H*FNR(30)):REM HUNTERS EAT NUTS
920 IFF>7000THENF=F-(H*FNR(30)):REM AND SOME FRUIT
930 RETURN
940 REM TEMPORARY ANIMAL DATA
950 T1=BR:T2=DR:T3=RC:T4=RF:T5=RB:T6=TD:T7=I:T8=F:T9=N
960 RETURN
970 T1=BR-T1:T2=DR-T2:T3=RC-T3:T4=RF-T4:T5=RB-T5
980 T6=TD-T6:T7=I-T7:T8=F-T8:T9=N-T9
990 RETURN
995 REM SET UP MONTHLY TOTALS
996 B1=INT(BR):B2=INT(DR):B3=INT(RC):B4=INT(RF):B5=INT(RB)
997 B6=INT(TD):B7=INT(I):B8=INT(F):B9=INT(N)
998 RETURN
1000 GOSUB1140:GOSUB970
1005 PRINT"    BEARS:        ";INT(T1)
1010 PRINT"    DEER:         ";INT(T2)
1020 PRINT"    RACCOON:      ";INT(T3)
1030 PRINT"    RED FOX:      ";INT(T4)
1040 PRINT"    RABBIT:       ";INT(T5)
1050 PRINT"    TOADS:        ";INT(T6)
1055 PRINT"HIT ANY KEY TO CONTINUE"
1060 GETZZ$:IFZZ$=""THEN1060
1070 ZZ$=""
1080 RETURN
1100 INPUT"[O]PEN OR [C]LOSE HUNTING SEASON";H$
1110 IFH$="C"THENRETURN
1120 IFH$="O"THENINPUT"HOW MANY HUNTERS THIS YEAR";H
1130 RETURN
1140 IFBR<0THENBR=0
1145 BR=INT(BR)
1150 IFDR<0THENDR=0
1155 DR=INT(DR)
1160 IFRC<0THENRC=0
1165 RC=INT(RC)
1170 IFRF<0THENRF=0
1175 RF=INT(RF)
1180 IFRB<0THENRB=0
1185 RB=INT(RB)
1190 IFTD<0THENTD=0
1195 TD=INT(TD)
1200 IFI<0THENI=FNR(100)+2
1205 I=INT(I)
1210 IFF<0THENF=FNR(100)+2
1215 F=INT(F)
1220 IFN<0THENN=FNR(100)+2
1225 N=INT(N)
1230 RETURN
```

18. One-Man Voyage

Your orders arrive via special courier: your skills as a pilot are needed to save a planet from certain doom. You have orders to transport an ultra-sophisticated computer to a distant world. This computer will aid in the preservation of the world's population. As it stands, thermonuclear war is imminent, unless the computer can be delivered in time.

Since time is of the essence, you are being asked to use the newest and fastest transport vehicle known. As a matter of fact, the ship is so new that construction has just been completed. All the defense units: photon missiles, lasers, shields, sensors, and computers have been installed. The only thing missing is the final programming; the programming which tells you which button makes what work.

As you ascend the lift to the command module, one of the scientists explains; "You have two modes; Auto defense and manual. In the manual mode, use the 0 to 9 keys. In the Auto-defense mode, you have to use the 'P' or 'L' keys for Photons or Lasers. Ship movement is done with the two keys labeled 'CRSR' and the one marked 'SHIFT'..."

Further explanations are cut off as the hatchway closes, cutting off communications. As you strap in, the onboard systems begin to hum. The computer only has one more bit of information for you; from then on, you're on your own!

PLAYING AND HELPFUL HINTS

The commands for the ETRAV's computer, in manual mode, are scrambled each time you play the game. By using the numeric keys (0-9), you can "call" the following sections:

A. Navigation Section 1: This section displays your present speed in Relative Fuel Units (an imaginary quantity between 0 and 10). You may change your speed by inputting a new value, or you may remain at the displayed speed by simply pressing the RETURN key.

B. Navigation section 2: This section displays the numerical coordinates which represent your ship's position in space. Since you are travelling in space, an imaginary three dimensional grid is used to reference your position. The NORTH coordinate represents your X axis, the EAST coordinate represents your Y axis, and the SECTOR number refers to the Z axis. See the figure below.

C. Status Report: This section displays the fuel level as well as the percentage of power available to the laser, photon, and shield devices.

D. Sensor Scan: This section shows computerized images of stars, planets, and unknown objects in the sector in which you are presently travelling.

E. Guidance Computer: By entering a "C" for CONTINUE, your on-board computer will automatically correct your course for you. When you reach sector ten, you must be at the pre-programmed coordinates in order to land.

F. Photon weapon: Fires one photon weapon in manual mode.

G. Laser: Fires one laser shot in the manual mode.

H. Defense Mode: Detects any enemies in your sector and displays fuel level as well as weapon and shield charges.

I. Landing Sequence: This section will allow you to land on the planet at the pre-programmed destination. Any attempt to land while not at the proper location will be cancelled.

Note: At all times, you are viewing a computer representation of events outside the ETRAV.

- Remember: use the 0–9 (numerical) keys in the manual mode.

- Use the "P" and "L" keys, along with the cursor and shifted cursor keys in the Auto-defense mode.

- It is helpful to slow down after a battle, both to re-charge your weapons and shields, and to re-calculate your heading.

- If sensors show no enemies in the first fractions of a sector, chances are that you can warp through at maximum speed at ten R.F.U. (relative fuel units).

- Once you identify the Photon and Laser keys in the manual mode, avoid using them, as this drains their power unnecessarily.

- Always use the course correction computer after a battle.

PROGRAM HIGHLIGHTS

A definitive description of the program would tend to give away the method for consistently winning the game. Therefore, I will point out the more interesting aspects of the program.

Lines 11000 to 11950 generate the sprite for the enemy craft. Line 11005 is a loop to skip over the first 45 datum from the data lines. These skipped lines are used to produce the theme song. Therefore, the sprite data is actually generated from the data in lines 11900 to 11950. Lines 1000–2030 are two interwoven subroutines which a) provide the theme music and b) print the title of the program, one character at a time, in step with the music. Line 2000 controls the printing of the title. Lines 2040–2080 are also two nested subroutines, providing the sound and graphics for the ship's lift-off sequence.

PROGRAM LISTING

```
1 Poke53281,11:gosub11000
4 Poke54276,0:Poke54283,0:dimcm$(11),sa$(280)
5 k$="    ExPerimental TransPort Vehicle          ":Printchr$(14)
8 deffnr(r2)=int(rnd(0)*r2)+1
10 Print"":gosub1004:Print:Print
20 inPut"       Please enter your name";na$:ti$="000000"
25 Pokes+4,0:Pokes+18,0:Print""
30 Print"             E T R A V                   "
31 Print"   ExPerimental TRAnsPort  Vehicle       "
32 fortc=1to10
33 Print"                                       "
34 next
35 Print"                                         "
36 Print"        Welcome aboard, CaPtain ";na$
37 Print"    We're sorry, but there wasn't"
38 Print"    time to Program the commands.":Print:Print
39 Print"    Press the 'S' key, followed "
40 inPut"    by the RETURN key ";c$
41 ifleft$(c$,1)="s"then45
42 Print"":goto30
45 Print"     PrePare for countdown: ";
50 forzz=10to0steP-1:forzx=1to850:next
55 Print"                                            ";zz
56 next
57 fortc=1to10
58 Print"                                       "
59 next
60 Print"                                         "
70 gosub2040:Print"        Switching to manual mode":gosub2090
75 fortc=2to11
76 cm$(tc)=str$(int(rnd(0)*10)+1)
77 fortx=1totc:ifcm$(tx-1)=cm$(tc)then76
78 nexttx
79 nexttc:Print"":fortx=1to10:cm$(tx)=cm$(tx+1):next
80 rem ****set uP variables
81 fx=fnr(10):fy=fnr(10):fd=10
82 hx=0:hy=0:hd=1:f=500:Pc=100:lc=100:sc=100:sP=0
83 gosub5000:sc=sc+1:ifsc>100thensc=100
84 Print"      Command __"
85 getc$:ifc$=""thengosub5000:goto85
86 Print"           ";c$
87 if(asc(c$)<48)or(asc(c$)>57)then84
88 co=val(cm$(val(c$)+1)):Print""
89 oncogoto100,140,190,205,290,350,400,500,545,205
90 goto84
100 Print"      Navigation, Section 1:"
110 gosub10000
120 Print:Print"     Present sPeed:";sP;" R.f.u"
125 inPut"NEW SPEED ";sP
130 goto83
140 Print"      Navigation, Section 2:"
150 gosub10000
160 Print:Print"    Present heading:"
165 Print"      ";hx;" East, by ";hy;" North. Sector ";hd
170 Print"    NEW HEADING:"
175 inPut" Enter East, North coordinates";hx,hy
180 goto83
190 Print"      ETRAV Status RePort:"
195 gosub10000
```

```
200 print"Fuel level: ";f;" units.
201 print"Photon chg: ";pc;" %"
202 print"Laser  chg: ";lc;" %"
203 print"Shield chg: ";sc;" %"
204 goto83
205 print"█████████ETRAV Sensor Scan"
206 gosub10000:f9=0
210 ty=25*int(hd):print"████Sector: ";hd
215 print"█████"
216 print"████████████████████ ———— █"
220 forly=1to25step5
230 print"██████████████";
235 print"██ █ ";
240 forlx=1to5
250 printsa$(lx+ty+ly);:ifsa$(lx+ty+ly)="█E"thenf9=f9+1
260 next:print"██ █"
270 next:print"███████████████████ ———— █"
280 print"E= ";f9:goto83
290 gosub5290:goto83
350 gosub5350:goto83
400 print"████████████Guidance Computer"
410 gosub10000
415 print"████Final Destination Programmed:"
420 print"███";fx;" East, by ";fy;" North, Sector ";fd
425 print"█████COMPUTED  OFFSET:"
430 print"███";fx-hx;"          ";fy-hy;"          ";fd-hd
435 input"  [R]eturn to Command or [C]ontinue";gc$
440 ifgc$="r"then83
445 ifgc$<>"c"thenprint"***INPUT ERROR***":goto470
446 iffx<hxthensx=-1
447 iffy<hythensy=-1
448 iffy>hythensy=1
449 iffx>hxthensx=1
450 fortx=hxtofx+(-1*sx)stepsx
451 forty=hytofy+(-1*sy)stepsy
455 print"████████████████Correction:"
460 print"████";tx;" East, by ";ty;" North"
465 next:next:hx=tx:hy=ty
470 goto83
500 print"████████████";:iff9=0thenprint"█";
501 iff9>0thenprint"█";
505 print"   Entering defense mode    "
506 print"**Sensors detect no enemies "
510 print"   █    Shields on; ";sc;" %"
515 print"       Laser chrg; ";lc;" %"
520 print"      Photon chrg; ";pc;" %"
525 print"      Fuel level; ";f;" units"
530 iff9>0thengosub5060
540 goto83
545 gosub6060:goto83
1000 rem "Game Theme"
1001 rem "Orion's Wake"
1002 rem "Music (C) Copyright 1982"
1003 rem "by Bill L. Behrendt"
1004 s=54272:mc=0
1010 pokes+24,175:pokes+5,15:pokes+6,31
1020 pokes+23,113:pokes+21,7:pokes+19,11:pokes+20,15
1030 readnl,vh,vl:ifnl=-1thenmc=mc+1:restore:goto1030
1035 pokes+4,33:pokes+18,1:pokes+1,vh:pokes,vl
1040 form=1tonl/6:pokes+22,peek(s+28):next:pokes+4,32:pokes+18,
1041 gosub2000
1045 ifmc<3then1030
```

```
50 restore:return
00 data 305,6,108,270,19,63,62,21,154,62,24,63,62,25,177
10 data 270,28,214,62,24,63,62,25,177,124,28,214,62,25,177
20 data 62,24,63,175,3,155,175,10,205,450,9,159,-1,-1,-1
00 cP=cP+1:P$=mid$(k$,1,cP)
10 Print"◆◆◆◆◆◆◆◆◆◆"
20 PrintP$;
30 return
40 s=54272:rem **blast off!**
41 Pokes+24,175:Pokes+5,15:Pokes+6,31
42 Pokes+23,113:Pokes+21,7:Pokes+19,255:Pokes+20,223
43 Pokes+12,255:Pokes+13,255
45 Pokes+4,17:Pokes+11,129:Pokes+18,1
46 fortc=1to255:gosub2060
47 Pokes+1,tc:Pokes,55:Pokes+8,tc/1.5:Pokes+7,55
48 Pokes+22,Peek(s+28):next
49 Pokes+4,16:Pokes+11,128:Pokes+18,0
50 return
60 iftc<100thenPrint"◆◆◆◆◆◆◆◆◆◆◆◆◆◆◆◆◆◆◆◆◆◆◆◆◆◆◆◆◆◆◆◆◆◆◆◆◆▶◆ ◆Engines ignited"
70 iftc>120thenPrint"◆◆◆◆◆◆◆◆◆◆◆◆◆◆◆◆◆◆◆◆◆◆◆◆◆◆◆◆◆◆◆◆◆◆◆◆◆◆◆◆ Lift off..        "
75 iftc>251thenPrint"◆◆◆◆◆◆◆◆◆◆◆◆◆◆◆◆◆◆◆◆◆◆◆◆◆◆◆◆◆◆◆◆◆◆◆◆◆◆◆◆◆                 "
80 return
90 fortc=1to280 :rem sa$(280)
00 tx=fnr(15)
01 iftx=1thensa$(tc)="◆*":rem star
02 iftx=2thensa$(tc)="◆O":rem Planet
03 iftx=3thensa$(tc)="*?":rem unknown
04 iftx=4thensa$(tc)="◆E":rem enemy
05 iftx>4thensa$(tc)="◆◆ ◆":rem sPace
06 next:Print"◆":goto10000
00 hd=hd+(.005*sP):f=f-(.05*sP)
01 hd=1000*hd:hd=int(hd):hd=hd/1000
02 f=1000*f:f=int(f):f=f/1000
03 iff<1thenPrint"◆◆◆◆◆◆◆◆◆◆◆◆Sorry, you're out of fuel":end
04 iff<100thenPrint"◆◆◆◆◆◆◆◆***Low Fuel***◆"
10 ifsP>10thenPrint" Speed f(";sP;") too high. ◆**Adjusting**◆":sP=10
15 ifhx<0thenhx=0
16 ifhy<0thenhy=0
17 ifhx>10thenhx=10
18 ifhy>10thenhy=10
20 Pc=Pc+1:ifPc>100thenPc=100
25 ifPc<30thenPf=1
30 lc=lc+1:iflc>100thenlc=100
35 iflc<30thenlf=1
36 iflc>80thenlf=0
37 ifPc>80thenPf=0
40 ifhd>10thenhd=10
41 if(hd=10)and(hx=fx)and(hy=fy)thenPrint"◆◆◆◆◆◆◆◆◆◆◆◆  Destination   ◆"
42 ty=25*int(hd)
43 forly=1to25steP5:forlx=1to5
44 ifsa$(lx+ly+ty)="◆E"thenkk=1:f9=f9+1
45 next:next
47 ifkk=1thenPrint"◆◆◆◆◆◆◆◆◆*Auto Defense Mode*◆◆":fortt=1to1000:next
48 ifkk=1thengosub6160:kk=0:gosub5060
49 ifkk=0thenf9=0
50 return
50 Print"◆◆◆   ———————WARNING: ENEMY ATTACKING———————":ht=0
51 hy=fnr(10):hx=fnr(10)
52 Poke53248,44:Poke53249,44
53 gosub12000
55 fortx=1to10:forty=1to10:Poke53281,2:next:Poke53281,11:next:Print"◆"
70 e4=int(rnd(0)*20)+100:Poke53269,1:e5=40
```

```
5075 e5=e5-fnr(5)+5
5076 e4=e4-fnr(5)+5
5077 ife5>200thene5=200
5078 ife4>200thene4=200
5079 ife4<25thene4=25
5080 ife5<25thene5=25
5081 poke53248,e4:poke53249,e5
5085 ifht=1thenf9=f9-1:iff9<1then5170
5086 ifht=1thenht=0:goto5070
5087 print"       enemies left ";f9
5090 getpl$:ifpl$=""thengosub6150:goto5075
5091 gosub12000
5100 ifpl$="p"thengosub5290:goto5075
5110 ifpl$="l"thengosub5350:goto5075
5125 ifpl$="▌"thene5=e5+fnr(20)-hd/3
5130 ifpl$="▌"thene4=e4+fnr(20)-hd/3
5135 ifpl$="▌"thene4=e4+fnr(20)-hd/3
5140 ifpl$="▌"thene5=e5-fnr(20)-hd/3
5150 ife4<25thene4=25
5155 ife5<25thene5=25
5160 ife4>200thene4=200
5165 ife5>200thene5=200
5167 goto5080
5170 print"       Enemies left ";f9:poke53269,0:poke53281,1
5175 gosub6000:poke53281,11:return
5289 stop
5290 s=54272:pokes+24,175:pokes+5,15:pokes+6,17
5291 pc=pc-20:ifpf=1thenprint"          photon recharging▌":retur
5292 ifpc<10thenpf=1
5295 pokes+23,113:pokes+21,7:pokes+19,21:pokes+20,193
5300 pokes+12,31:pokes+13,241
5305 pokes+4,21:pokes+11,129:pokes+18,1
5310 lp=1993:rp=2013
5315 fortc=10to1step-1
5320 lp=lp-39:rp=rp-41
5325 pokelp,95:pokerp,105:pokelp+39,32:pokerp+41,32
     :pokes+lp,95:pokes+rp,105
5330 pokes+1,tc*2:pokes,160:pokes+8,tc*4:pokes+7,60
5335 pokes+22,peek(s+28):next
5336 pokelp,42:pokerp,42:pokelp,32:pokerp,32
5340 pokes+4,20:pokes+11,128:pokes+18,0
5341 if(peek(53279)>0)and(e5>154)and(e4>110)thenht=1
5345 return
5350 s=54272:pokes+24,175:pokes+5,15:pokes+6,17
5351 lc=lc-20:iflf=1thenprint"          laser recharging▌":retur
5352 iflc<10thenlf=1
5355 pokes+23,113:pokes+21,7:pokes+19,21:pokes+20,193
5360 pokes+12,31:pokes+13,241
5365 pokes+4,129:pokes+11,21:pokes+18,1
5370 lp=1993:rp=2013
5375 fortc=10to1step-1
5380 lp=lp-39:rp=rp-41
5385 pokelp,94:pokerp,94:pokes+lp,95:pokes+rp,105
5390 pokes+1,tc*5.7:pokes,60:pokes+8,tc*9.45:pokes+7,10
5395 pokes+22,peek(s+28):next
5396 pokelp,42:pokerp,42:pokelp,32:pokerp,32:print"▌"
5397 pokes+4,128:pokes+11,20:pokes+18,0
5398 if(peek(53279)>0)and(e5>154)and(e4>110)thenht=1
5399 return
6000 pt=25*int(hd)
6010 forly=1to25step5
6020 forlx=1to5
6030 ifsa$(lx+pt+ly)="▌E"thensa$(lx+pt+ly)="▌  ▌"
```

```
6040 next:next
6050 return
6060 ifhd<>10thenprint"██████Not at programmed destination:"
6061 ifhd<>10thenprint"███Landing sequence cancelled":return
6062 s=54272:pokes+24,175:pokes+5,15:pokes+6,31
6063 pokes+23,113:pokes+21,7:pokes+19,255:pokes+20,223
6064 pokes+12,255:pokes+13,255
6065 pokes+4,33:pokes+11,129:pokes+18,1
6066 fortc=255to10step-1:gosub6080
6067 pokes+1,tc:pokes,55:pokes+8,tc/1.5:pokes+7,55
6068 pokes+22,peek(s+28):next
6069 pokes+4,0:pokes+11,0:pokes+18,0
6070 gosub1000:print"████████You've saved the planet!"
6075 pokes+4,0:pokes+11,0:pokes+24,0:end
6080 iftc<100thenprint"█████████  ██Engines off          "
6090 iftc>120thenprint"█████████ ██ Entering atmosphere"
6095 iftc>251thenprint"█████████ ██                     "
6100 return
6150 ne=fnr(10):ifne<7thenreturn
6160 print"███████Enemy has fired...":s=54272
6161 pokes+4,0:pokes+11,0:pokes+18,0
6165 pokes+24,175:pokes+8,5:pokes+7,125
6170 ts=fnr(2):ifts=1thents=129
6175 ifts=2thents=33
6180 pokes+23,195:pokes+21,7:pokes+19,19:pokes+20,199
6190 pokes+12,31:pokes+13,241:pokes+4,21:pokes+11,ts:pokes+18,1
6200 fortc=250to1step-25
6210 pokes+1,tc+1:pokes,100:pokes+8,(tc+1)/2:pokes+7,50
6220 pokes+22,peek(s+28)
6225 nexttc:pokes+11,21
6230 pokes+5,15:pokes+6,17:pokes+4,129:pokes+19,21:pokes+20,193
6231 pokes+18,1:pokes+23,113:pokes+24,175:pokes+21,7
6232 pokes+19,21:pokes+20,193
6233 fortz=255to1step-25
6234 pokes+1,4:pokes,23
6235 pokes+22,peek(s+28)
6236 poke53281,1
6237 poke53281,11
6238 nexttz:pokes+4,128:pokes+18,0:pokes+11,0
6239 print"███████                      "
6240 sc=sc-5:print"█████████Shield chg:     █████";sc;" ██ %"
6250 ifsc<5then7000
6260 return
7000 s=54272:rem explosion
7010 pokes+24,175:pokes+5,15:pokes+6,31
7020 pokes+23,113:pokes+21,7:pokes+19,21:pokes+20,207
7030 pokes+12,31:pokes+13,255:pokes+4,21:pokes+11,129:pokes+18,1
7040 fortc=15to1step-.25
7050 poke53281,tc:pokes+1,fnr(150):pokes,fnr(150)
7060 pokes+8,fnr(150):pokes+7,peek(s+28)
7070 pokes+22,peek(s+28)
7080 next
7090 pokes+4,20:pokes+11,128:pokes+18,0
7100 print"█":end
10000 print"████████TIME ACCESSED: ";left$(ti$,2);":";
10010 printmid$(ti$,3,2);":";right$(ti$,2):return
11000 v=53248:poke2040,200
11005 fortt=1to45:readd:next
11010 fortc=0to62:readd:poke12800+tc,d:next
11015 restore
11020 return
11900 data0,0,0,0,0,0,0,0,0,16
```

```
11910 data16,16,56,16,56,111,255,236,56,124
11920 data56,16,124,16,0,254,0,0,254,0
11930 data1,255,0,3,255,128,7,255,192,15
11940 data255,224,127,255,252,127,255,252,97,255
11950 data12,96,124,12,96,16,12,0,0,0,0,0,0
12000 s9=fnr(400):poke1424+s9,46:poke55696+s9,1
12010 s9=fnr(400):poke1424+s9,32
12015 s9=fnr(400):poke1424+s9,32
12020 s9=fnr(400):poke1424+s9,32
12025 s9=fnr(400):poke1424+s9,32
12030 s9=fnr(400):poke1424+s9,32
12035 s9=fnr(400):poke1424+s9,32
12040 s9=fnr(400):poke1424+s9,32
12045 s9=fnr(400):poke1424+s9,32
12050 s9=fnr(400):poke1424+s9,32
12055 s9=fnr(400):poke1424+s9,32
12100 return
```

ok

MODIFICATIONS

To make the game more difficult, change line 5000 thus:

$$5000 \ hd - hdt + (.005*sp):f = f - (.25*sp)$$

This will cause the ETRAV to use fuel at a faster rate.

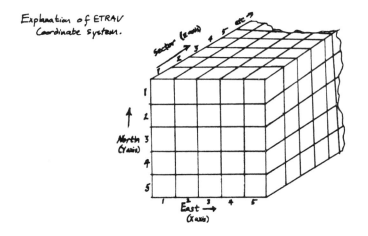

Explanation of ETRAV
Coordinate System.

19. Mutation Maker

A mutation is, generally, a change, or deviation, in cellular structure or composition from one generation to the next. This change is sometimes drastic, sometimes subtle. In any case, the mutation can be either beneficial or disastrous. If the mutation causes the offspring to have an advantage over non-mutated species, the mutated variety will survive in places where the non-mutant would die out.

This program began as a simulation of a mutation's effect on the laws of natural selection (survival of the fittest). By the addition of user-selected cell groupings, however, it becomes playable as a game. The goal of the game is to come up with a group of cells which can, via mutation, survive the onslaught of various environmental changes.

CELL TYPE	USE
@	"@" KEY
▨	"B" WITH COMMODORE KEY
▨	"+" WITH COMMODORE KEY
◯	"W" WITH SHIFT KEY
⬤	"Q" WITH SHIFT KEY
⊞	"E" WITH COMMODORE KEY
◢	"£" WITH SHIFT KEY

After the cells have been input, the computer will begin displaying each eon, and its type of environment. The program will continue until all cells have disappeared. To stop the program prematurely, use the RUN/STOP key.

PROGRAM HIGHLIGHTS

Line 5 seeds the random number generator. After changing the background to white, the program calls the subroutine beginning at line 1000, to display the cell selection menu.

After returning to line 10, where the cell input counter is reset to zero, the inputting of cells begins. A quick programming trick was used to convert ASCII values to screen display codes. After the cell is input to a string, it is briefly PRINTed in the upper left of the screen. This corresponds to screen memory location 1024. This location is then PEEKed, to obtain the proper screen display code. Lines 40–45 accomplish this. The subroutine beginning at line 1500 is used to determine the correct color for each cell.

Following the input of the ten cells, lines 55–70 clear the top 19 lines of the screen memory. Line 80 is the beginning of the main program section; ET holds a random number, which will determine the Eon Type. Lines 81–89 decode and display the present eon environment.

The heart of the program is in the loop between lines 90 and 380. This area of the program compares the environment types with each of the cell types and determines the proper outcome for the cell. The cell will either reproduce (lines 400–405), die (lines 500–506), mutate (lines 600–601 and 700–707), or will remain dormant (in which case, the computer will fall through to line 380 for the next iteration of the loop).

After all ten cells have been taken care of, the program calls the subroutine at lines 800–840. This subroutine counts the remaining cells. If no cells are left, the program halts.

If the program is to continue, it will return to line 390, from which it goes on the line 80 to determine the next EON.

PROGRAM LISTING

```
5 W=RND(-TI):G9=INT(RND(0)*10)+10
10 POKE53281,1:GOSUB1000:Y=0
20 PRINT"■CELL INPUT"
30 FORX=1870TO1888STEP2:Y=Y+1
35 PRINT"■ЖЖЖЖЖЖЖЖЖЖЖЖЖЖЖЖЖCELL #";Y;:
   INPUT"TYPE";A$(Y)
36 PRINT"ЖЖЖЖЖЖЖЖЖЖЖЖЖЖЖЖЖЖЖЖ                    "
40 PRINT"■◄■";A$(Y)
45 POKEX,PEEK(1024):GOSUB1500
46 POKEX-40,PEEK(1024):GOSUB1500
50 NEXTX:PRINT"⬛"
55 FORX=1TO19
60 PRINT"                                       "
70 NEXT
80 ET=INT(RND(0)*7)+1:EO=EO+1:PRINT"EON";EO
81 IFET=1THENE$="π▨DESERT"
82 IFET=2THENE$="▮RAIN FOREST"
83 IFET=3THENE$="▨ICE AGE"
84 IFET=4THENE$="▨ACID RAIN"
85 IFET=5THENE$="▨VOLCANIC"
86 IFET=6THENE$="▮SEASONAL"
87 IFET=7THENE$="■SUNLESS"
88 PRINT"ЖЖЖЖ                                  "
89 PRINT"ЖЖЖЖ";TAB(15);E$
90 FORX=1870TO1888STEP2
91 G9=INT(RND(0)*10)+10
95 CT=PEEK(X)
100 IF(ET=1)AND(CT=87)THENGOSUB400:GOTO380
110 IF(ET=1)AND(CT=113)THENGOSUB600:GOTO380
120 IF(ET=1)AND((CT=0)OR(CT=81))THEN380
130 IFET=1THENGOSUB500
```

```
140 IF(ET=2)AND(CT=127)THENGOSUB400:GOTO380
150 IF(ET=2)AND(CT=0)THENGOSUB600:GOTO380
160 IF(ET=2)AND((CT=105)OR(CT=81)OR(CT=102))THEN380
170 IFET=2THENGOSUB500
180 IF(ET=3)AND(CT=102)THENGOSUB400:GOTO380
190 IF(ET=3)AND(CT=81)THENGOSUB600:GOTO380
200 IF(ET=3)AND((CT=127)OR(CT=105)OR(CT=113))THEN380
210 IFET=3THENGOSUB500
220 IF(ET=4)AND(CT=105)THENGOSUB400:GOTO380
230 IF(ET=4)AND(CT=127)THENGOSUB600:GOTO380
240 IF(ET=4)AND((CT=0)OR(CT=87))THEN380
250 IFET=4THENGOSUB500
260 IF(ET=5)AND(CT=0)THENGOSUB400:GOTO380
270 IF(ET=5)AND(CT=105)THENGOSUB600:GOTO380
280 IF(ET=5)AND(CT=87)THEN380
290 IFET=5THENGOSUB500
300 IF(ET=6)AND(CT=81)THENGOSUB400:GOTO380
310 IF(ET=6)AND(CT=102)THENGOSUB600:GOTO380
320 IF(ET=6)AND((CT=127)OR(CT=113))THEN380
330 IFET=6THENGOSUB500
340 IF(ET=7)AND(CT=113)THENGOSUB400:GOTO380
350 IF(ET=7)AND(CT=87)THENGOSUB600:GOTO380
360 IF(ET=7)AND(CT=102)THEN380
370 IFET=7THENGOSUB500
380 NEXT:GOSUB800
385 FORZQ=1TO999:NEXT:REM THIS 'WAIT' LOOP MAY
    BE ALTERED TO TASTE
390 GOTO80
400 AX=X
401 AX=AX-40:IFAX<1224THEN405
402 IFPEEK(AX)<>32THEN401
403 POKEAX,PEEK(X)
404 POKEAX+54272,PEEK(X+54272)
405 RETURN
500 IFINT(RND(0)*G9)+1<9THENRETURN
501 BX=X:GOTO503
502 BX=BX-40:IFBX<1224THENBX=BX:GOTO504
503 IFPEEK(BX-40)<>32THEN502
504 POKEBX,32:POKEBX+54272,1
505 RETURN
600 IFG9>=15THENRETURN
601 GOSUB700
607 CX=X+40
608 CX=CX-40:IFCX<1224THENCX=CX:GOTO630
609 POKECX,PV:POKECX+54272,CV
610 IFPEEK(CX-40)<>32THEN608
620 CX=CX+40:IFCX<>X+80THEN620
630 RETURN
700 IFCT=0THENPV=127:CV=5
701 IFCT=127THENPV=105:CV=4
702 IFCT=102THENPV=81:CV=3
```

```
703 IFCT=87THENPV=113:CV=0
704 IFCT=81THENPV=102:CV=6
705 IFCT=113THENPV=87:CV=7
706 IFCT=105THENPV=0:CV=2
707 RETURN
800 FORX=1870TO1888STEP2
810 IFPEEK(X)=32THENEF=EF+1
820 NEXT:FORZZ=1TO2500:NEXT
830 IFEF<10THENEF=0:RETURN
840 IFEF=10THENPRINT"    ALL CELLS DEAD":END
1000 PRINT"           C E L L S   I"
1005 PRINT"                                        "
1010 PRINT"        DESERT: = |X|X|*|=|=|↑|X|"
1020 PRINT"RAIN FOREST:|↑|*|=|X|=|X|=|"
1030 PRINT"       ICE AGE: X|=|*|X|↑|=|=|"
1040 PRINT"     ACID RAIN:|=|↑|X|=|X|X|*|"
1050 PRINT"      VOLCANIC: *|X|X|=|X|X|↑|"
1060 PRINT"     SEASONAL:|X|=|↑|X|*|=|X|"
1070 PRINT"      SUNLESS: X|X|=|↑|X|*|X|"
1080 PRINT:PRINT:PRINTTAB(14);"   KEY:
1090 PRINTTAB(5);"   *  OR *: CELL MULTIPLIES"
1100 PRINTTAB(5);"   =  OR =: CELL IS DORMANT"
1110 PRINTTAB(5);"   X  OR X: CELL DIES"
1120 PRINTTAB(5);"   ↑  OR ↑: CELL MUTATES"
1130 PRINT"         0 1 2 3 4 5 6 7 8 9"
1140 RETURN
1500 IFA$(Y)="@"THENC=2
1510 IFA$(Y)="."THENC=5
1520 IFA$(Y)="※"THENC=6
1530 IFA$(Y)="o"THENC=7
1540 IFA$(Y)="●"THENC=3
1550 IFA$(Y)="⊥"THENC=0
1560 IFA$(Y)="▼"THENC=4
1570 POKEX+54272,C
1575 POKEX+54232,C
1580 RETURN
```

The effect each Eon Type has upon each of the cell types.

Eon Type	Cells which die	Cells which Multiply	Cells which Mutate	Cells which remain dormant
Desert	◣■▼	o	⊥	@ ●
Rain Forest	o ⊥	◣	@	■ ● ▼
Ice Age	@ o	■	●	◣ ⊥ ▼
Acid Rain	■ ● ⊥	▼	◣	@ o
Volcanic	◣ ■ ● ⊥	@	▼	o
Seasonal	@ o ▼	●	■	◣ ⊥
Sunless	@ ◣ ● ▼	⊥	o	■

20. Demon's Lair

Your muscles are stretched to the breaking point. A wall is behind you; another wall is to your right. To your left is the long, cramped corridor through which you've just come. In front of you is the only way left to go.

As you peer at the door for some type of handle, your head begins to spin. Suddenly, lighter than air, you feel your body passing through the door. Involuntarily, you raise your sword, and make ready with your knife. After a few frantic moments, you find the door behind you, and a fierce goblin in front of you. Fangs dripping, foul breath steaming, the goblin advances upon you. You begin swinging your sword and flailing with the knife. Seconds later, the dead goblin is lying prone over a pile of gold. You roughly kick aside the body and scoop the coins into your girdle. Peering around the room, you realize that this is the final unmapped room. Having completed this level, you touch the magic medallion, and are whisked through time and space to land on the next plane of existence. Your journey has barely begun.

This program, as you can see from the listing, is quite long. However, I'm sure you'll find it worth the effort to type in. With this program, you can explore an endless variety of dungeons. (Actually, there are only 1,235,520 possible combinations.)

One of the interesting points of the program is that the dungeon is revealed as you go through it. The walls, treasures, etc. will not be visible until you walk within lantern range of them. They will remain lit, once you've discovered them.

Another point of interest is that the program was written in such a manner as to retain the secrets and surprises you'll find along the way. Even the method by which the dungeon is designed is in coded form. This way, you can type in the program, without really knowing what the final outcome will be. This introduces an element of discovery and surprise, not usualy found in printed programs, but usually only possible in ready to go games found on cartridge, tape and disk.

PLAYING

After RUNning, the theme music will begin, and the logo will appear. To start the game, hold down the SPACE bar until the logo disappears. At this point, the computer will begin constructing the dungeon. This process may take as long as 45 seconds (remember, there are over a million possible dungeons!). To alert you that the dungeon is almost complete, the computer will generate random tone sequences for about ten seconds before displaying your initial position.

Figure 1:

Space - open area

◻️ -wall or obstacle

◊ -treasure

Ⓜ -monster

◤ -Door

◉ -Player

Figure 1 shows the various symbols used to represent the dungeon. When your initial position is shown, you'll notice a white band near the bottom of the screen. This is given as a reference point, and shows the bottom-most line of the dungeon. The solid white circle is your present position.

As you move around in the dungeon, the eight blocks surrounding the player marker are shown. If one of the symbols is within this area, it will be displayed; open areas remain black (see figure 2).

Figure 2:

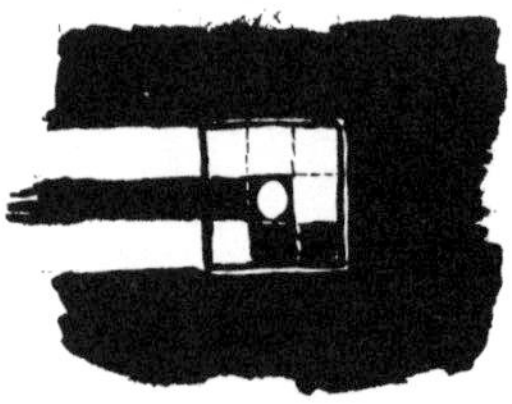

The eight blocks around the player are shown.

ENCOUNTERS

Encounters with the various symbols are handled differently. If you see a treasure, it may be guarded by a hidden monster. The only way to find out is to move over the treasure symbol. Your take will be shown, if you recover the treasure. If the treasure is guarded, your player marker will become invisible for a short time, and the monster type will be displayed.

To engage in battle with the monsters, you have two control keys. Use the "K" key to stab with your knife, the "S" key to swing your sword. Each monster is weaker against *one* of these weapons. As the battle is in progress, the player marker will show which weapon is being used. At the top of the screen will be two numbers. The MONSTER number will decrease with every hit. When you bring the Monster's number down to zero, the monster is dead. Meanwhile, the monster is attacking you, and if your number falls below one, you will "die." The trick, during battles, is to determine which weapon is most effective and to use that weapon against the enemy.

When encountering doors, you will occasionally come up to a locked door, through which you can not pass. Treat it as befits a warrior.

Walls, generally, cannot be passed through. However, certain of the monsters have special magical powers which can pull you through solid objects.

One word of advice: don't always believe what you see!

SECRET HINTS

1: Look closely at dirty walls.
2: Good things come in small packages.
3: Look for the Greek headdress.
4: Look for the King's hat.
5: The good effects from one dungeon do not stay with you when you move to the next level.

FINAL WORDS

To move around the dungeon, use these keys:

"J"—move right
"H"—move left
"U"—move up the screen
"N"—move down the screen
"R"—"Get me out of here!" (moves you to the next dungeon.)

PROGRAM LISTING

```
1 POKE53281,0:W5=RND(-TI):PRINT"⌑":GOSUB1300
2 DEFFNR(R0)=INT(RND(0)*R0)+1:CA=54272:SF=0:PS=50:RP=0
3 M$(1)="CNROOTNEILLEBKOSG":M$(2)="LNLEOBRETKTAANRS":ZF=ZF+TF
4 M$(3)="FPLEORWIYPMMMAUVM":TF=0:PRINT"⌑"
5 DA=1147:PA=1510:PRINTCHR$(144)
6 PRINT"▨          ◪                                  ▆"
7 GOSUB1000:RP=0:X=0:X1=0:Y=0:MZ=0
10 FORX=1TO6
11 F=FNR(13)
12 ONFGOSUB5000,5005,5010,5015,5020,5025,5030,5035,5040,5045,
      5050,5055,5060
15 FORY=1TO3:DA=DA+40
20 FORX1=1TO30:GOSUB1340
21 POKEX1+DA+CA,0
22 K=ASC(MID$(D$(Y),X1,1))-35
23 IFK=1THENPN=160
24 IFK=0THENPN=32
25 IFK=2THENPN=77
26 IFK=3THENPN=13
27 IFK=4THENPN=90
28 IFK=5THENPN=96:SF=SF+1:IFSF>7THENSF=3:PN=32:GOTO30
29 IFK=6THENPN=224:SF=SF+1:IFSF>5THENSF=3:PN=32:GOTO30
30 POKEX1+DA,PN
40 NEXTX1,Y,X:POKE53280,FNR(15):POKEV+21,0
45 PRINT"▩◖◖◖◖◖◖◖◖◖◖◖◖◖◖◖◖◖◖◖◖◖◖◖◖◖◖◖    ◪
50 POKEPA,81:POKEPA+CA,1:POKEPA+40+CA,1:POKEPA+41+CA,1:POKEPA+39+C▮
55 POKEPA-40+CA,1:POKEPA+CA-41,1:POKEPA+CA-39,1
56 POKEPA+CA-1,1:POKEPA+CA+1,1
57 GOSUB720
60 GETA$:IFA$=""THEN60
65 POKEPA,32:IFTF>500THEN3
70 IFA$="U"THENPA=PA-40:GOSUB150
80 IFA$="N"THENPA=PA+40:GOSUB150
85 IFA$="R"THEN3
90 IFA$="J"THENPA=PA+1:GOSUB150
95 IFA$="H"THENPA=PA-1:GOSUB150
100 GOTO50
150 IFPEEK(PA+1)=13THENPA=PA+1:POKEPA+CA,5
155 IFPEEK(PA+41)=13THENPA=PA+41:POKEPA+CA,5
160 IFPEEK(PA-1)=13THENPA=PA-1:POKEPA+CA,5
165 IFPEEK(PA-41)=13THENPA=PA-41:POKEPA+CA,5
170 IFPEEK(PA+40)=13THENPA=PA+40:POKEPA+CA,5
175 IFPEEK(PA+39)=13THENPA=PA+39
180 IFPEEK(PA-40)=13THENPA=PA-40
185 IFPEEK(PA-39)=13THENPA=PA-39
190 IFPEEK(PA)=32THENRETURN
200 IF(A$="U")AND(PEEK(PA)=160)THENPA=PA+40:RETURN
210 IF(A$="N")AND(PEEK(PA)=160)THENPA=PA-40:RETURN
215 IFA$="R"THEN3
220 IF(A$="J")AND(PEEK(PA)=160)THENPA=PA-1:RETURN
230 IF(A$="H")AND(PEEK(PA)=160)THENPA=PA+1:RETURN
240 SD=FNR(2)
250 IFPEEK(PA)<>77THEN310
260 IFSD=1THENRETURN
270 IF(A$="U")AND(PEEK(PA)=77)THENPA=PA+40:RETURN
```

```
280 IF(A$="N")AND(PEEK(PA)=77)THENPA=PA-40:RETURN
290 IF(A$="J")AND(PEEK(PA)=77)THENPA=PA-1:RETURN
300 IF(A$="H")AND(PEEK(PA)=77)THENPA=PA+1:RETURN
310 IFPEEK(PA)<>90THEN340
315 PRINT"                                        "
316 TF=TF+FNR(35)
320 PRINT"  TOTAL TREASURE: ";TF;"COINS"
330 RETURN
340 IFPEEK(PA)<>13THEN640
350 O=FNR(3):OP=FNR(3)
360 IFO<>1THEN390
370 IFOP=1THENMH=17:ML=7
375 IFOP=2THENMH=16:ML=2
380 IFOP=3THENMH=5:ML=1
390 IFO<>2THEN410
395 IFOP=1THENMH=16:ML=8
400 IFOP=2THENMH=15:ML=11
405 IFOP=3THENMH=9:ML=1
410 IFO<>3THEN440
420 IFOP=1THENMH=17:ML=9
425 IFOP=2THENMH=16:ML=4
430 IFOP=3THENMH=7:ML=1
440 DM$="  "
445 FORMC=MHTOMLSTEP-2
450 DM$=DM$+MID$(M$(O),MC,1)
460 NEXT
465 PRINT"                                        "
470 PRINT"       MONSTER: ";DM$
480 LP=FNR(10+O+RP)
490 FORTC=1TO500:NEXT
500 WS=FNR(2+RP)
510 FM=FNR(2+RP)
530 IFLP<=0THENLP=0:GOTO620
531 POKEPA+CA,1:IFPS>0THEN539
535 IFPS<=0THENPS=0:PRINT"           YOU HAVE FAILED
    YOUR MISSION!"
536 PRINT"TOTAL TREASURE THIS GAME: ";ZF:PRINT:
    PRINT"PLAYER STATUS: ";DL$
538 STOP
539 PRINT"                                        "
540 PRINT"  CREATURE:    ";LP;" PLAYER       ";PS
550 GETC$:FORTC=1TO(RP+1)*50:NEXT:IFC$=""THEN590
560 IFC$="S"THENLP=LP-FM:POKEPA,19
570 IFC$="K"THENLP=LP-WS:POKEPA,11
580 GOTO530
590 PS=PS-2:POKEPA+CA,2:PS=PS+(INT(RP/2))
600 GOTO580
620 PRINT"  CREATURE:    ";LP;" PLAYER       ";PS
630 FORTC=1TO2500:NEXT:PRINT:PRINT:PRINT"":RETURN
640 IFPEEK(PA)=96THENS9=FNR(2):GOTO650
645 IFPEEK(PA)=224THENS9=FNR(2)+2:GOTO650
646 RETURN
650 SP$(1)="ABBBUXFTMFVSNLB"
655 SP$(2)="BCAPLSYMFQTOTCHEO"
660 SP$(3)="ABASBGSFBKJLUX"
665 SP$(4)="BBCHUBILPLKJTBLB":PT$=""
670 T1=LEN(SP$(S9))-(ASC(MID$(SP$(S9),3,1))-64)
675 T2=ASC(MID$(SP$(S9),2,1))-64
```

```
680 FORS5=T1TO4STEP-T2
685 PT$=PT$+CHR$((ASC(MID$(SP$(S9),S5,1))-64)-
      (ASC(MID$(SP$(S9),1,1))-64)+64)
690 NEXT
691 PRINT"       "
695 PRINT"   YOU HAVE FOUND THE ";PT$;" OF ";DL$
700 RP=RP+1:ZL=ZL+(LEN(PT$)):IFZL>=210THENPRINT
      "   YOU'VE SAVED THE KINGDOM!":END
710 RETURN
720 LL=PEEK(PA+1):L9=1:GOSUB810
730 LL=PEEK(PA-1):L9=-1:GOSUB810
740 LL=PEEK(PA+40):L9=40:GOSUB810
750 LL=PEEK(PA-40):L9=-40:GOSUB810
760 LL=PEEK(PA-41):L9=-41:GOSUB810
770 LL=PEEK(PA+41):L9=41:GOSUB810
780 LL=PEEK(PA-39):L9=-39:GOSUB810
790 LL=PEEK(PA+39):L9=39:GOSUB810
800 RETURN
810 IFLL=160THENL8=15
820 IFLL=77THENL8=12
830 IFLL=13THENL8=LL
840 IFLL=90THENL8=10
850 POKEPA+L9+CA,L8
860 RETURN
900 PRINT"":STOP
1000 V=53248:POKEV+21,3:POKEV+39,1:POKEV+40,1
1005 RESTORE
1010 POKE2040,175:POKE2041,176:L0=L0+1:PRINT"   LEVEL:";L0
1015 IFL0>0THENDL$="SILVER"
1016 IFL0>2THENDL$="GOLD"
1017 IFL0>4THENDL$="POWER"
1018 IFL0>6THENDL$="HEALING"
1019 IFL0>8THENDL$="MAJIK"
1020 POKEV,122:POKEV+1,115:POKEV+2,170:POKEV+3,115
1030 POKEV+23,3:POKEV+29,3
1040 FORTC=0TO62:READD:POKETC+11200,D:NEXT
1050 FORTC=0TO62:READD:POKETC+11264,D:NEXT
1060 GETBG$:S9=FNR(15):POKEV+40,S9:POKEV+39,S9
1065 FORTC=1TO100:NEXT:GOSUB1460:GETBG$
1070 IFBG$=""THEN1060
1080 POKEV+21,0:RETURN
1100 DATA 240,30,198,72,32,170,68,64,146
1110 DATA 66,248,162,68,69,130,72,32,130
1120 DATA 240,30,130,0,0,0,0,32,24,0,32,36
1130 DATA 0,32,34,0,32,62,0,62,34
1140 DATA 0,0,0,56,94,243,68,210,148
1150 DATA 186,82,144,162,94,241,186,66,146
1160 DATA 68,68,148,56,88,247
1170 DATA 24,133,143,36,133,144,66,196,160
1180 DATA 130,165,24,68,148,6,40,140,1
1190 DATA 16,140,62,0,0,62,60,0
1200 DATA 8,34,0,8,60,0,8,40,0
1210 DATA 62,38,0,0,0,0,30,62,120
1220 DATA 145,0,4,145,0,4,21,32,120
1230 DATA 21,32,64,21,16,64,149,14,64
1231 DATA 0,0,0,0,97,51,100,20,177,25,0,0
1232 DATA 0,0,0,0,97,51,100,20,177,25,0,0
1233 DATA 0,0,0,0,97,51,100,20,177,25,0,0
```

```
1234 DATA 0,0,0,0,198,45,100,20,177,25,200,40
1235 DATA 0,0,0,0,126,38,70,15,227,22,0,0
1236 DATA 0,0,0,0,126,38,70,15,227,22,0,0
1237 DATA 0,0,0,0,126,38,70,15,227,22,0,0
1238 DATA 0,0,0,0,75,34,70,15,227,22,141,30
1239 DATA 0,0,0,0,75,34,100,20,56,27,0,0
1240 DATA 0,0,0,0,75,34,100,20,56,27,0,0
1241 DATA 0,0,0,0,75,34,100,20,56,27,0,0
1242 DATA 0,0,0,0,126,38,100,20,56,27,75,34
1243 DATA 63,19,177,25,94,32,63,19,177,25,94,32
1244 DATA 63,19,177,25,94,32,63,19,177,25,94,32
1245 DATA 63,19,177,25,94,32,63,19,177,25,94,32
1246 DATA 63,19,177,25,94,32,63,19,177,25,94,32
1300 SD=54272:POKESD+24,79:POKESD+5,31:POKESD+6,251
1305 DIMM$(3),D$(3)
1310 POKESD+12,31:POKESD+13,251
1320 POKESD+23,199:POKESD+19,31:POKESD+20,251
1330 RETURN
1340 MZ=MZ+1:IFMZ<500THENRETURN
1350 IFK=0THENWZ=33:WX=33:WY=33
1360 IFK=1THENWZ=33:WX=21:WY=129
1370 IFK=2THENWZ=21:WX=129:WY=33
1380 IFK=3THENWZ=17:WX=129:WY=21
1410 IFK>3THENWZ=21:WX=21:WY=21
1420 POKESD+5,WZ:POKESD+11,WX:POKESD+18,WY
1425 POKESD+1,FNR(120)
1426 POKESD,FNR(120)
1427 POKESD+8,FNR(120)
1428 POKESD+7,FNR(120)
1429 POKESD+15,FNR(120)
1430 POKESD+14,FNR(120)
1435 POKESD+22,FNR(120)
1440 POKESD+5,0:POKESD+11,0:POKESD+18,0
1450 RETURN
1460 SD=54272:RESTORE:FORTC=1TO126:READD:NEXT
1470 FORTC=1TO28
1480 READD2,D1,D4,D3,D6,D5
1485 POKESD+1,D1:POKESD,D2:POKESD+8,D3:POKESD+7,D4
1486 POKESD+15,D5:POKESD+14,D6
1487 POKESD+4,33:POKESD+11,33:POKESD+18,33
1488 POKESD+22,234
1490 FORNL=1TO150:NEXT
1495 POKESD+4,32:POKESD+11,32:POKESD+18,32
1500 NEXT
1505 FORNL=1TO208:NEXT
1510 POKESD+4,0:POKESD+11,0:POKESD+18,0
1520 RETURN
5000 D$(1)="$##$#$#$#$#$#$#$%$$$%$$##$%$$%$$"
5001 D$(2)="$#####$'$##$$#$###$###$###$###$$"
5002 D$(3)="$##$#$$$####$#'$#$#&#$'&#######$"
5003 RETURN
5005 D$(1)="$#######$#$#$######$###$%$$##$$###"
5006 D$(2)="$##$####$##$#####'&####&##&#$$$"
5007 D$(3)="$#####$#$'#$#'##########'###$$"
5008 RETURN
5010 D$(1)="$######$$'%%#&'##########$########$"
5011 D$(2)="$###########&'$$$$####$####'%$$"
5012 D$(3)="$%%&'########$#'#$###$$###$###$$$"
```

```
5013 RETURN
5015 D$(1)="$##´##%$$$$$$####´##&$$#&##&$$"
5016 D$(2)="$&###($###$##$##$´%#####$$#####$"
5017 D$(3)="$#####´##%´&$$$##########$###$$$"
5018 RETURN
5020 D$(1)="$#########$####$######&$$####$$$"
5021 D$(2)="$#´%######$##$###)%#####$#$$$$$"
5022 D$(3)="$###&´´##%´$$$$$$%###$######$$$"
5023 RETURN
5025 D$(1)="$###$##$###$##$##&##%#$###%##%###$"
5026 D$(2)="$##´&####$######$##$##$#######$"
5027 D$(3)="$#########$$#######%#######$$#####$"
5028 RETURN
5030 D$(1)="$###$######$###$##$%$$$$%#$$$$$"
5031 D$(2)="$####´&###$####%##%##%###$$$$$"
5032 D$(3)="$#########$$$$$$%$$$$$$$$$$$$"
5033 RETURN
5035 D$(1)="$#####################%$$$$$$"
5036 D$(2)="$#####´&#$$&#&#&%´#´#´##´&$$$$$"
5037 D$(3)="$#########$$%$$%$%$$%$%$%$$$$$"
5038 RETURN
5040 D$(1)="$####$$%$$%####´#´###$######$$"
5041 D$(2)="$#(##&#&$$&#############$$$$$$"
5042 D$(3)="$#####$$$$######&´#########$$$$"
5043 RETURN
5045 D$(1)="$$#####$%$$%$#$$$$´$´$$$###%´&$$"
5046 D$(2)="$$$)$´$&#$###$$###$%$$$$$$$$$$"
5047 D$(3)="$$#####$##$$$##&´#$$$####$$$$"
5048 RETURN
5050 D$(1)="$##$%$$####´($$$&####&´##%$$$$"
5051 D$(2)="$#######$###$$##$$##########$###$$"
5052 D$(3)="$$$%$$$####$#######&##´$#$´#####$"
5053 RETURN
5055 D$(1)="$%%$$$$´´´´´($$$$###########$$$$"
5056 D$(2)="$#(##´%#$()###&$###$#&´$#$###$$"
5057 D$(3)="$$%%$$$$#######################$"
5058 RETURN
5060 D$(1)="$######$´##########$#$#$#$$$$$$$"
5061 D$(2)="$###$%#%#$$$$##$$##$##$#$###$$$"
5062 D$(3)="$$####$$##$####$###$###$####$$$"
5063 RETURN
```

APPENDIX

DESCRIPTION OF CONTROL CODES IN QUOTE MODE
—UPPER CASE

CURSOR CONTROLS:

"◼" -- CURSOR DOWN

"◼◼" -- CURSOR RIGHT

"◻" -- CURSOR UP

"◼◼" -- CURSOR LEFT

"◻" -- CLR/HOME (CLEAR SCREEN & HOME CURSOR)

"◼" -- HOME CURSOR (SCREEN IS NOT CLEARED)

FUNCTION KEYS:

"◼" -- F 1

"◼" -- F 2

"◼" -- F 3

"◼" -- F 4

"◼◼" -- F 5

"◼" -- F 6

"◼◼" -- F 7

"◼" -- F 8

COLOR COMMANDS:

"■" --- BLACK

"◀" --- WHITE

"▩" --- RED

"◣" --- CYAN

"▨" --- PURPLE

"▐▌" --- GREEN

"▦" --- BLUE

"▥" --- YELLOW

"▞" --- ORANGE

"◤" --- BROWN

"▩" --- LIGHT RED

"▩" --- DARK GREY

"▩" --- MEDIUM GREY

"▮▌" --- LIGHT GREEN

"▟" --- LIGHT BLUE

"▐▌" --- LIGHT GREY

"▨" --- REVERSE ON

"▬" --- REVERSE OFF

DESCRIPTION OF CONTROL CODES IN QUOTE MODE
—LOWER CASE

Cursor controls:

"▤" -- cursor down

"▐▌" -- cursor right

"▨" -- cursor up

"▌▌" -- cursor left

"▨" -- clr/home (clear screen & home cursor)

"▤" -- home cursor (screen is not cleared)

Function keys:

"▤" -- f1

"▐▌" -- f2

"▤" -- f3

"▐▌" -- f4

"▨" -- f5

"▨" -- f6

"▐▌" -- f7

"▤" -- f8

Color commands:

"█" -- black

"�" -- white

"█" -- red

"▓" -- cyan

"▟" -- purple

"▐" -- green

"▒" -- blue

"✦" -- yellow

"▜" -- orange

"▙" -- brown

"▛" -- light red

"▐" -- dark grey

"▞" -- medium grey

"▛" -- light green

"▙" -- light blue

"▓" -- light grey

"▜" -- reverse on

"▟" -- reverse off

NOTES

NOTES